Passover

The Festival of Redemption

Understanding the Jewish roots of our faith is a golden key that unlocks the treasures of Holy Scripture and enriches Christian lives. This fundamental concept is the focus of Hebraic Christian Global Community, an international, transdenominational, multicultural publishing and educational resource for Christians.

Hebraic Christian Global Community features individuals and congregations who share the vision for restoring Christianity's Hebraic foundations, for networking together in true community, and for returning the church to a biblical relationship of loving support for the international Jewish community and the nation of Israel.

We publish ***Restore!*** magazine, a high-quality journal featuring theological balance and scholarly documentation that helps Christians recover their Hebrew heritage while strengthening their faith in Jesus.

We also publish ***Hebraic Insight***, a quarterly Bible-study journal that assists individuals, families, study groups, and congregations in inductive Hebraic study of the Scriptures that is accurate, balanced, and trustworthy.

We also distribute books from ***Golden Key Press*** in order to disseminate high quality teaching about Christianity's Hebraic foundations that is non-threatening and non-judgmental and helps believers grow in Christian understanding.

We also provide various media resources through ***New Treasures*** media productions. Many of these can be accessed on our website.

The ministry of Hebraic Christian Global Community is made possible by our many partners around the world who share in our ***Golden Key Partnership*** program. We invite you to join us in sharing the satisfaction of knowing that you are a partner in an organization that is making a difference in the world by restoring Christians to their biblically Hebraic heritage, by eradicating Judaeophobia and anti-Semitism, by supporting Israel and the international Jewish community, and by encouraging collaborative efforts among those who share this vision.

For information about Hebraic Christian Global Community and all our resources and services, contact us at:

HEBRAIC CHRISTIAN GLOBAL COMMUNITY
P.O. Box 421218
Atlanta, Georgia 30342, U.S.A.
www.HebraicCommunity.org

Passover

The Festival of Redemption

John D. Garr, Ph.D., Th.D.

P.O. Box 421218
Atlanta, Georgia 30342, U.S.A.

Published by Golden Key Press
P. O. Box 421218, Atlanta, GA 30342
ISBN 978-0-9794514-6-1

Printed in the United States of America

All Scripture verses are quoted from the
New American Standard Version
unless otherwise noted.

TABLE OF CONTENTS

Introduction

Since the time in the third century when controversy arose in the Christian church over whether or not Christians should associate their celebration of the resurrection of Jesus with Passover, millions of Christians have been deprived of a very important historical and theological aspect of their faith. For the first three centuries, most of the church continued to observe the resurrection on the Sunday after Passover. By the time of the fourth century, however, the Western Church (Roman Catholicism) had outlawed this practice, and by the eleventh century, the Eastern Church (Greek Orthodoxy) had followed suit.

This action by the two major divisions of historical Christianity was the product of growing Judaeophobia and Antisemitism that eventually came to characterize the entire Christian church. The official church determined that it was necessary to sever its historical and theological connection with the Jews and Judaism so it changed the time of Resurrection Sunday from the actual day of the Festival of Firstfruits on the Jewish calendar to the first Sunday after the full moon following the vernal equinox on the

Julian calendar. Because of these sweeping actions by the church's councils and clergy, Christianity was wrenched from its moorings in the safe harbor of Hebraic truth and practice and was set adrift in a maelstrom of human tradition. The faith practices of Yeshua and his Jewish apostles were abandoned in favor of times and traditions that overlapped pagan festivals and even incorporated some of their symbols and practices. Because of these aberrations of ecclesiastical history, millions of Christians from that time forward were literally robbed of the legacy of Jesus and the apostles and deprived of the richness of their biblical heritage.

Amazingly, the two events that form the foundation of all Christian faith, the death and resurrection of Jesus, were uprooted from their historical and theological context and were transplanted into soil that was foreign to the land and the people of the Bible. The memorial of Jesus' death was changed from the very day of Passover to what became known as "Good Friday." The remembrance of Jesus' resurrection was changed from the very day of Firstfruits to what became known as "Easter Sunday." In the process, the rich context of Jesus' death and resurrection was obscured at best and obliterated at worst.

It is reasonable to conclude that Jesus' commandment to his disciples to "remember" his death until he returns by sharing the elements that he distributed to them on the night before he died also includes making the memorial of his crucifixion coincide with the day of Passover. There is no legitimate reason for any change to be made in the timing of its celebration. In truth, it was the rabid anti-Judaism and Antisemitism that infected the church at the time of the third century that prompted such actions. The church became hell-bent on defining itself as "not Jewish," and in so doing, it violated the most fundamental of Messianic ceremonial requirements, remembering Christ's death until he comes at the time when history and Scripture prove that these events occurred.

In this scenario, it became easy for Christians to caricature Jews as "Christ killers" and to call for their persecution and murder. The Jewish people even came to dread the church's annual Good Friday celebrations because they often became occasions for Christians to engage in acts of violence against them. The church of Jesus actually became the enemy of the family of Jesus! This historical tragedy, which was based on the church's official supersessionism and its determination to change days and seasons, reached profound proportions during and after the Dark Ages.

THE TIMES, THEY ARE CHANGING

After centuries of bad news for both the Jews and the church, a new day has begun to dawn in the Christian church at large. Though official Christianity often frowns on or downright condemns "Jewish" practices, the good news is that increasing numbers of Christians around the world are beginning to recognize the historical church's error in ripping the most sacred events of salvation history out of their biblically Hebraic matrix and connecting them with pagan celebrations. These Christians are reconnecting with the Passover event and with its proper timing. A reformation of restoration is underway that is destined to alter the Christian landscape by making Christianity what it was always intended to be, the Jewish faith of Jesus and the apostles. This represents what one secular newsmagazine termed one of the major sea changes on the world scene today.

In order to assist the millions of Christians who are

already embracing Passover as central to their faith and to introduce millions more to this important aspect of biblical religion, I have undertaken to write this volume. In it, I discuss the historical and theological truths about Passover's Jesus connection. In so doing, I provide a spiritually enriching context for the death, burial, and resurrection of our Lord so that these pivotal events of human history can be understood to be in complete continuity with and foreshadowed by events that occurred fifteen hundred years before that time.

In this book, I also provide worship outlines designed to include both Jewish orders and language as well as Christian form and tradition. Any of these may be modified, expanded, or condensed according to your need or preference. The purpose of these outlines is to help Christian families, Bible study groups, home fellowships, and congregations celebrate Passover in a manner that is consistent with the observance that Jesus and the earliest Jewish and Gentile Christians enjoyed and to do so in ways that accommodate their own Christian understandings and traditions.

First, I offer a complete Christian Passover Haggadah, including the various features that have long been common to Jewish Passover observances. This *Seder* (order) includes various traditional blessings in Hebrew with accompanying transliterations and English translations. The leader of your Passover celebration may choose to omit the Hebrew, using the English translations instead.

Second, I offer a commentary and a Passover Haggadah that is limited to the elements of the traditional Jewish Passover *Seder* which we know Jesus and the apostles observed when they celebrated the Last Supper. This is an abbreviated version of the complete Passover Haggadah which can be more easily celebrated in a traditional Christian corporate worshipping settings where time constraints might make the traditional *Seder* seem laborious and time-consuming.

Third, I offer a New Covenant Passover celebration, a Liturgy for Holy Communion. This ceremony features some elements of the synagogue liturgy that was a part of the life experience of both Jesus and the apostles. It also employs language commonly used in that time for blessings, including the blessing to God for the elements of communion, the bread and the fruit of the vine. This Liturgy for Holy Communion can be used in any congregational setting, especially those with sacramental and liturgical traditions.

I would like to express my personal thanks to my colleagues Dr. Marvin R. Wilson, Dr. Karl D. Coke, and Dr. Dwight A. Pryor (of blessed menory) for their invaluable assistance in the development and production of this book. I am also deeply indebted to Judy Grehan both for excellent input into the manuscript and for careful editing of the text. Then, my sincere appreciation goes to my friends Zvi Zachor and Yuval Shomron for their encouragement and help in the production and the marketing of this book.

Passover observance in which both the Exodus event and the Calvary experience are celebrated is foundational to Christian faith. The very first Passover is a part of Christian salvation history, a foundational event in the unbroken chain of deliverance that eventuated in the manifestation of Yeshua, the Messiah and Savior of the world. The very first Passover of the New Covenant era is most assuredly essential to Christian faith, for it was on this day that the Son of God, the Son of man, offered himself on the cross for the redemption of humanity.

Answers to the question of why Christians would want to observe Passover with traditional Jewish forms and language should be apparent. If these worship experiences were important to Jesus and his disciples (and it is beyond doubt that they were), they should certainly be of great import to those who assert that they are "like Christ" by calling themselves "Christians." The question of Passover observance for Christians, then, is not "Why?" but "Why not?"

The choice is ours. Is Passover observance essential to salvation? No! Salvation is grounded solely in our faith in Jesus; therefore, Passover observance can never been seen as a salvation exercise. It is, however, a worship exercise, an opportunity to offer pure, biblically sound praise and adoration to the heavenly Father for the unmerited gift of his unfathomable grace in sending his only begotten Son into the world that all men might be saved and inherit the gift of eternal life.

Christians are not required to observe Passover; however, they certainly have the liberty to do so. Passover is an annual appointment to remember God's redemption, first of Israel, and then of all mankind. It is an opportunity to fulfill the command of Jesus that believers "remember his death" until he returns. Because Christ our Passover has been sacrificed for us, let us, therefore, observe this festival with the unleavened bread of sincerity and truth by turning away from the errors of historical Christianity and embracing the original faith of Jesus Christ.

Fraternally in the Messiah
John D. Garr, Ph.D., Th.D.
Purim 2012

Chapter 1

Christians and Passover

In Leviticus 23, God himself enumerated what he called, "*my* feasts," and then he enjoined their observance upon his chosen people *forever*. From this action alone, it is clear that God supports and sponsors annual remembrance celebrations of the great events of salvation history. Indeed, the fact that God himself scheduled those events to coincide with the appointed times on his calendar indicates that even he observes his own festivals! There is not the slightest doubt that when God became human in the person of Yeshua, our Savior commemorated both the Torah and post-Torah festivals of his people, the Jews, including the Festival of Passover.

The purpose and nature of all the festival celebrations of Scripture is revealed in the Hebrew word that is translated "festival." The word *chag* means to dance or twirl in a circle in ecstatic joy. No somber, ominous, morose, lachrymose events, these divinely ordained festivals! While the gods of the pagans kept their subjects in fear and torment, dreading some capricious, vengeful act of retribution, the Eternal always expected his subjects to be filled with joy whenever they assembled with him his convocations.

A PEOPLE OF WORSHIP AND SERVICE

The unbridled, God-intoxicated emotion of the Jewish people in their joyful worship of God continued into the earliest church, as is evidenced by the recorded events of the first Pentecost following Christ's ascension. These Jews—Jesus and his apostles—were free to celebrate the goodness of God's provision, for they understood that everything God had created was "very good" (Genesis 1:31). Passover for them was not a sad, foreboding exercise. It was a joyous celebration. The apostles understood what millions of subsequent Christians should have known too: "Christ our Passover has been sacrificed for us." On the same day on which God had effected the children of Israel's deliverance from Egyptian bondage, these Jewish believers in Yeshua rejoiced in God's provision for the deliverance of the entire world from the bondage of sin and death. They understood that God had made that provision by the same means by which he had effected the Exodus: by the sacrifice of the paschal lamb, in this case, "the Lamb of God who takes away the sin of the world" (John 1:29).

The earliest Christians experienced "joy unspeakable and full of glory" (1 Peter 1:8) when they gathered annually on the very day of Passsover to fulfill their Lord's commandment that they remember his death until he comes (1 Corinthians 11:26). Their joy was further augmented by the fact that they knew Jesus' death was merely the precursor of his resurrection. They had the privilege of recognizing and worshipping the Lord Jesus who rose from the dead as the firstfruits of the resurrection on the same day that their ancestors had celebrated the Feast of Firstfruits (Leviticus 23:10-14). Then, fifty days later, as they celebrated the giving of the Torah, they received the infilling of the Holy Spirit—again on the very same day on which the Torah had been given at Sinai: "When the day of Pentecost had fully come" (Acts 2:1-4).

First-century believers had no apprehensions or reservations about God's liturgial calendar. They knew that it was outlined in his Word (Exodus 23:16), and they knew that their ancestors had faithfully observed it for fifteen centuries or more. As a matter of fact, they understood that their calendar was a significant part of their distinctiveness and separation from the rest of the world. Their religion was focused on God-designed and God-ordered liturgical practices carried out at God-specified times called *mo'edim* ("appointments") in Hebrew. They had daily (Hours of Prayer), weekly (Sabbath), monthly (New Moon), annual (Seven Festivals), and generational (*Shmita* Year and Year of Jubilee) events on their calendar that were designed to reinforce their remembrance of their God and the faith that he had given them.

The apostles even conducted their lives in accordance with God's calendar. At Jesus' bidding, all of them were in Jerusalem when the Day of Pentecost "was fully come," and they were then baptized with the Holy Spirit along with the rest of the first Christian community (Acts 2:1-4). Peter and John witnessed a great miracle when they went to the Temple "at the hour of prayer" (Acts 3:1). Paul was diligent about being in Jersualem for Pentecost (Acts 20:16), and he set his appointment calendar by the festivals (1 Corinthians 16:8). As a matter of fact, when he left Ephesus, he told his colleagues, "I must by all means keep this feast that is coming in Jerusalem" (Acts 18:21).

As the church became increasingly Gentile in leadership and demographics, however, political, social, and religious pressures gradually diminished its Hebrew consciousness, which was replaced with Greek rationalism. Days and seasons were changed to accommodate nationalist sensibilities. God's holy days were sacrificed in favor of man's appointed celebrations. A rich legacy of biblical tradition was soon buried under the encroaching sands of human tradition, depriving millions of Christians of their biblical heritage. The seasonal clarion calls of remembrance of God's mighty acts were silenced. Rich symbolism that ever rehearsed and clarified mature relationships with God faded into oblivion. Christians were left deprived of clear pictures of the living Christ that for centuries had been painted annually in the chosen festivals of the Hebrew Scriptures.

JESUS AND THE REFORMED FAITH

Neither Jesus nor his apostles ever suggested that the system of faith and practice that God had delivered to his people Israel should be abolished, superseded, or replaced. For them to have done so would have been unthinkable, for it would have represented rebellion against what they knew to be truth as God himself had established it. They stood firmly on the foundation of truth that had been revealed to prophets and sages who were "carried along by the Holy Spirit" (2 Peter 1:21) such that their declarations were not even influenced by their own interpretation of what God had said. They simply reported what had been revealed to them as accurately as they possibly could. What they reported was, therefore, "God-breathed" Holy Scripture (2 Timothy 3:16).

Simply stated, Jesus was a reformer, not an innovator. He did not come to destroy an antiquated, lifeless religion of legalism and bondage and replace it with a new, vibrant religion of mercy and peace. He came to fulfill the faith of the Hebrew Scriptures by "filling it full" with his own presence and completing it with the sacrifice that would forever perfect God's plan of salvation. Jesus affirmed this truth in his own words: "Do not think that I came to abolish the Law or the Prophets; I did not come to abolish but to fulfill. For truly I say to you, until heaven and earth pass away, not the smallest letter or stroke shall pass from the Law until all is accomplished. Whoever then annuls one of the least of these commandments, and teaches others to do the same, shall be called least in the kingdom of heaven; but whoever keeps and teaches them, he shall be called great in the kindgom of heaven" (Matthew 5:17-19).

As the living Word, the "Word made flesh," Jesus never deviated from the written Word of God. He taught only from the Law, the Prophets, and the Writings that comprise the Hebrew Scriptures (Luke 24:44). He always validated from the pages of Scripture what he was sent by the Heavenly Father to do (John 5:36; 10:25). Jesus was not a renegade mystic or a cynic philosopher, and he certainly was not a false prophet who would have enticed the people of God to abandon God's Word (Deuteronomy 18:20-22). He himself confessed that he had faithfully kept all of his Father's commandments (John 15:10). From this confession alone, it is clear that Jesus fulfilled without fail God's commandments relating to festival observance.

BECOMING MORE CHRISTIAN—MORE LIKE JESUS

Those who "want to be more like Jesus every day" will endeavor to do the things that Jesus did. Jesus was not, as one children's Sunday School quarterly recently described him, "a nice Christian boy who went to church every Sunday." He was a "nice Jewish boy" who went to "synagogue" every Sabbath, as his custom was (Luke 4:16)! In no way did Jesus seek to distance himself from the faith of his fathers according to the flesh, nor did he seek to distance himself from the faith of his heavenly Father that he as the immanent God had revealed to the Jewish prophets and sages centuries before his birth.

The good news is that God will ever labor to restore what is important to his plan for man. And nothing could be more essential to the Almighty than a growing, mature, ongoing relationship of loving devotion with his chosen people. Indeed, "The Father seeks such" (John 4:23). It is for this reason that the Holy Spirit has moved to bring about a restoration of God's appointment calendar so that his people may meet with him on his appointed days.

RESTORING BIBLICAL FAITH AND PRACTICE

The words of the earliest apostle to the Gentiles now echo and resonate in the hearts of millions of believers worldwide: "Christ our Passover is sacrificed for us; therefore, let us observe the festival . . . with the unleavened bread of sincerity and truth" (1 Corinthians 5:7-8). God's festivals are pregnant with meaning for those who embrace them, and they open the door to intimacy with the Divine at his appointed times. Observing them neither secures nor maintains one's status with God, for righteousness or right relationship with God is only by grace through faith in the shed blood of Jesus (Ephesians 2:8). Worship, however, should be that which is done in Spirit and in truth, carried out in the focused intensity of the Holy Spirit and in the accuracy and order of the revealed Word of God (John 4:23). It is high time to apply this principle to the Christian observance of Passover. Only when the church returns to sound biblical practice will it experience the richness of its heritage with and among the Jewish people of antiquity and the present day.

Chapter 2

One God: Two Miracles, Two Peoples, Two Faiths

Passover is a perpetual memorial of two pivotal events that are foundational to the two religions that represent the one God of Scripture, Judaism and Christianity. Each time a Torah-observant Jew or a Bible-believing Christian celebrates the Passover, he is calling to remembrance one or both of history's greatest episodes, the Exodus experience and the Calvary event. Without the Exodus, there would be no Jewish people. Without both the Exodus and Calvary, there would be no Christianity. As Anthony Saldarini has rightly observed, "Passover lives on in both the Jewish and Christian communities as a central ritual which expresses each community's identity and nature" (*Jesus and Passover,* Paulist Press, 1984, p. 4). The very essence of both Judaism and Christianity is manifest in the miraculous acts of God that occurred on the day of Passover. Without Passover, neither faith would have a foundation.

Passover marks two of the most momentous times

in history when the rectilinear path of divine providence intersected the plane of human need, times when the Eternal took the sovereign initiative to solve the woefully twisted enigma of human suffering. In one divine miracle of Passover deliverance, God brought forth a nation of perhaps two million Jews from one of history's most onerous slaveries, establishing for all succeeding generations the hope of the divine imperative: "Let my people go!" (Exodus 5:1). Fifteen centuries later, in yet another Passover miracle, the all-loving, all-knowing Father provided his Son as a Passover Lamb whose death on the cross established the atonement by which human sin could be passed over by divine love and mercy.

Immediately after the Passover event which produced Israel's Exodus from Egypt, God commanded the Israelites to celebrate the Passover each year forever (Exodus 12:14). He considered remembering the details of his miraculous deliverance so important that he established excommunication from the Israelite nation and from the presence of God as the penalty for failure to observe Passover (Exodus 12:15). For Israel's first fifteen hundred years, both the linear descendants of Jacob's sons and the unknown numbers of Gentiles who chose to embrace God's covenant with Israel observed the commandment.

It was entirely ordinary, then, that Jesus and his disciples shared the Passover meal on the evening before his death, and it was natural that Jesus himself used the elements of that meal to establish a New Covenant Passover ritual for all those who would come to faith in his name. This is why, as Samuele Bacchiocchi said, "No other religious ritual better reveals the organic relationship that exists between Judaism and Christianity than the Passover meal partaken of and transformed by Jesus into the very symbol of His redemption" (*God's Festivals in Scripture and History, Part 1, the Spring Festivals*, Biblical Perspectives, 1995, p. 32).

Passover and the Exodus

God commanded his chosen people to observe Passover throughout all their generations so that they might remember that their very existence as a people was wholly attributable to his gracious act of deliverance. Every Israelite in subsequent history was to declare during the course of his annual celebration of the Passover, "I was a slave in Egypt," maintaining the indelible impression that not only were his ancestors delivered from slavery but in a very real sense, he himself was likewise liberated. Individual

freedom is not the result of an accident of history: it is the product of God's lovingkindness and the miracle of his deliverance.

How could all the Jewish people who will ever live have been present in ancient Egypt and later at Mt. Sinai? The same principle was applied by the writer of the Book of Hebrews to say that "Levi paid tithes to Melchizedek while he was still in the loins of Abraham" (Hebrews 7:9-10). This time-honored Hebraic principle establishes the fact that continuity exists not only with what God does among his people but also within the people of God themselves. From generation to generation, God's mighty acts of history continue to impact his chosen people.

The enslaved Israelites' ancestors had come to Egypt as celebrities after Joseph had been positioned by divine providence in a place where he would be used by God to save not only the chosen people but all of Egypt as well. As a result of a divine gift that gave him insight into Egypt's future, Joseph was exalted by Pharaoh to be Egypt's prime minister. He was given the task of devising and implementing a plan to prepare for the seven years of famine which he had predicted in his interpretation of Pharaoh's dreams. During that time, he was also given charge over the distribution of the food that had been stored up during seven previous years of plenty.

As time progressed, the seventy family members who came with Joseph into Egypt multiplied to the point that the Egyptian authorities began to fear the power of their numbers. A Pharaoh "who knew not Joseph" (Exodus 1:8) began to enslave the Israelites, forcing them to work in deplorable conditions to build the architectural wonders of Egypt.

Faced with no prospect for relief, the Israelites cried

out to God for deliverance in an agonizing petition for liberation from the bitterness of their oppression. In order to underscore the miraculous provisions of his providence, God purposed to send a deliverer with a divine plan to liberate his enslaved people. God was preparing to fulfill the terms of his covenant with Abraham, and he had to secure the freedom of the Israelites in order to accomplish that task (Genesis 15:13-14).

At a time when Pharaoh had ordered all male Israelite newborn males to be drowned in the Nile River, a resourceful daughter of Israel hid her son for the first three months of his life. Then she directed her daughter Miriam to place the infant Moses in a basket made of reeds and with faith in God to set the little boat afloat on the Nile River. The small craft drifted directly to the place where one of Pharaoh's daughters was "coincidentally" bathing.

The princess of Egypt immediately had compassion on the baby, fell in love with him, and adopted him as her own son. She unwittingly engaged the child's own mother as his nurse. Thus, a slave baby was positioned in the imperial house where he acquired the world's best education, political power, and personal wealth. Despite the riches of Egypt that were lavished upon him by a doting adoptive mother, Moses could not escape his true patrimony: he was a son of the very slaves who were being exploited by the Egyptian pharaohs (Hebrews 11:26).

After a time when Moses was forty years of age, his suppressed anger erupted as he witnessed one of his people being severely beaten by an Egyptian taskmaster. Enraged with indignation, he came to the man's defense and, in the process, killed the taskmaster. Then, when he realized that his actions had been observed, he fled into the remote Sinai desert in order to escape possible retribution from the

Egyptian authorities.

For forty years Moses passed his time as a shepherd in the arid, difficult landscape. One day as he passed the barren slopes of Mount Sinai, out of the corner of his eye he caught a glimpse of a bush that was burning (not an unusual sight in this desert of scorching heat where bushes of this type often undergo spontaneous combustion). What riveted Moses' attention to this bush was the fact that despite the intense flame that encompassed it, the bush was not consumed.

When Moses "turned aside to see" this phenomenon, he positioned himself directly in the path of God's voice that called to him, "Moses, Moses." The Eternal God who spoke from the burning bush commissioned Moses to return to Egypt with a fateful message for Pharaoh: "Let my people go." Moses would not, however, secure Israel's liberty through his skills in diplomacy. By this time, he was suffering from a speech impediment that limited his effectiveness in communication. Perhaps because of this impediment, God equipped his prophet with the power to call forth miracles that would attest to the divine authority of his commands for Pharaoh. His shepherd's staff became "the rod of God" which produced many miracles.

God's plan was simple: speak to Pharaoh the words of the divine imperative and then be a channel for the display of awesome power. Ten plagues were devised by the hand of the Almighty to bring progressively more painful suffering to the land of Egypt in order to punish the obduracy of its leader. Interestingly, each of these plagues was also designed to demonstrate the God's judgment against Egypt's gods. To the amazement of the Egyptians in particular and perhaps of even most of the children of Jacob, the land of Goshen where the enslaved Israelites lived, was spared the withering effects of virtually all of the plagues. In Goshen, there were no swarming creatures, no dying cattle, no boils, no hail, no locusts, and no darkness.

The final and most devastating of the plagues targeted the Egyptian idolatry wherein Pharaoh and his son were worshipped as incarnate deities. God's judgment was that the firstborn of everyone in the land of Egypt was to be destroyed as the Lord himself passed through the land. The major difference between this concluding plague and its predecessors would be the fact that this time, Goshen would not escape the visitation of this night of terror.

In order to prepare the Israelites and provide a way of escape for their firstborn, God gave Moses a simple plan: on the fourteenth day of the first month, each of the families of Israel was to sacrifice an unblemished lamb at the threshold of their house. In an open display of disrespect for heathen gods, the lamb was sacrificed in the basin at the threshold of the door of each home. Then, the patriarch of each family dipped a piece of hyssop in the blood at the threshold and applied it conspicuously to both doorposts and to the lintel of the door, in effect completely encircling the door with the blood. "When I see the blood," God said, "I will pass over you." The Hebrew word for "pass over" is *pesach*, which literally means "to jump over." Marking the entry to each house with blood from the paschal lamb provided a way of escape for the Israelite firstborn because God would "jump over" their houses when he saw the blood.

It is interesting that God chose to have the lamb sacrificed at the threshold of the door of every Israelite household. This was in defiance of the ancient custom of pagan societies that placed a significant penalty (even death) upon anyone who stepped on the threshold of the entrance to a house or temple. Pagan peoples were superstitious about evil consequences that might occur if one stepped on the threshold. In this case, God had the lamb sacrificed right at or on the threshold of the door and its blood applied in a fashion that completed the encirclement of the door.

A second part of the requirement for escape was that the families were to remain in their houses throughout the night of the Passover, eating the roasted lamb, consuming bitter herbs, and sharing in bread that was made without yeast. The bread was the "bread of affliction," but it was also the "bread of haste" because there was not enough time to allow it to rise. After a seemingly interminable duration of suffering in slavery, God was going to do a quick work to bring his people out.

The Israelites awoke the following morning to find their firstborn spared. The Egyptians, on the other hand, were devastated, for the firstborn of every house, including that of Pharaoh, had died. In desperation Pharaoh's hardened heart finally relented, and he ordered the Israelites to leave Egypt. Throughout that day, the chosen people requested and received from the Egyptians gold and silver (equivalent to fair wages for the time of their slavery). Then, on the fifteenth day of the first month of the year, they departed from Egypt "with a high hand," knowing that God himself had delivered them.

The route that God chose for their escape was one which brought them face to face with the Red Sea. (The term *Red Sea* is a misnomer. It is actually the Reed Sea, *Yam Suph* in Hebrew). By that time, Pharaoh had reconsidered the liberation of the Israelites and had determined to retake them. The entire camp of Israel found itself confronted by the choice of death in the Red Sea or at the hand of Pharaoh's army. Moses, however, calmly ordered, "Stand firm and see the salvation of God!" Suddenly a powerful east wind began to blow, clearing a path of dry ground at the bottom of the sea. The walled-up sea stood at attention, forming a channel through which the Israelites could pass.

At that moment, each individual had to make a choice through an act of faith to cast his own life into the hands of the God who had parted the waters. All the Israelites walked down the western shore of the Red Sea believing that they would arrive alive on the eastern shore. Paul later characterized this act of faith as a baptism unto Moses, an immersion that came to be recognized as a death, burial, and resurrection to a different legal status. Just as centuries later proselytes to Judaism were forensically changed from strangers to Israelites when they emerged from the waters of the *mikveh* (baptism), so the Israelites experienced a change of status when they passed through the Red Sea. On the other side, they were no longer slaves but free people. They had passed through death to a new life of liberty

What was to be fulfilled in this new nation of believers in the God of creation would ever be founded upon that one eventful night in Egypt when God provided the lamb as a vicarious and efficacious atonement, a means of escape that secured their freedom. And, to ensure that each generation would not forget what God had done, the Lord decreed that every Israelite family would forever celebrate the Passover each year by eating the roasted lamb, the bitter herbs, and the unleavened bread. Every Israelite was instructed to celebrate the Passover as a virtual reenactment of the original event wherein one could relive the Passover in a very personal way. The first of the year for the Israelites would not be just the occasion of Spring when everything is renewed; it would be the time of redemption, the time of freedom. For them, everything began anew with Passover, the festival of redemption.

A SECOND PASSOVER, A REFORMED FAITH

For fifteen centuries, the Israelites had faithfully observed God's commandment by celebrating the Passover each year with their families and friends. In one such celebration, a group of Torah-observant Jews gathered around their Rabbi in a rented banquet room on an upper level near the temple compex. The Rabbi had said, "I have desired to celebrate this Passover with you before I suffer," as he had instructed his disciples to prepare for the Passover (Luke 22:15). When they gathered together that evening, he led them as they systematically followed the *seder* of observance that the sages of previous generations had prescribed. They ate the roasted lamb, dipped their unleavened bread in the bitter herbs (John 13:26), and sang the *Hallel* Psalms (Matthew 26:30).

This was the scene on the eve of Passover when *Yeshua HaMashiach* shared his last Passover celebration with his twelve disciples. During this Passover, however, Jesus instituted a New Covenant celebration for Passover that would forever be a memorial to demonstrate his death until his return. "Take, eat; this is my body," he declared of the unleavened bread. "Drink ye all of it; this is the new covenant in my blood," he said of the Passover wine. For the first time, they celebrated the momentous deliverance that was to occur on the very next day when the Lord was to consummate Jesus' role as "the Lamb of God who takes away the sins of the world," as John the Baptizer had described him three years earlier (John 1:29).

At the conclusion of the *seder*, these Passover celebrants went out to the Mount of Olives. There Jesus prayed for

hours in the Garden of Gethsemane near the Kidron Valley. All that was human in him cried out to his Father for release from the bitter cup of suffering that he would have to endure the following day. Finally, however, he uttered those immortal words of submission, "Not my will but thine be done." Just then, his betraying disciple, leading a band of men from the high priest, kissed him on the cheek, delivering him into the hands of his enemies.

During that night and early the following morning, Jesus was taken before various civil and religious authorities, none of whom could find fault in him. Just as the Passover lamb was to be "without blemish" (Exodus 12:5), so Jesus "offered himself without blemish to God" (Hebrews 9:14) so that all who would believe in him would be purified and presented "without blemish before the presence of his glory with rejoicing" (Jude 1:24). Even though he had no sin or guilt, the political conspiracy between the Roman civil authorities and some of the aristocratic, apostate religious leaders condemned Jesus to death. He was led outside the city of Jerusalem to a spot called the Place of the Skull, Golgotha, where he was nailed to the cross he had carried and crucified for all to see, the Son of God suspended between heaven and earth, the spotless Lamb of God bleeding and dying for the sins of the world.

On this momentous Passover, at the moment when the Son of God declared, "It is finished," and surrendered his last breath, the massive curtain of the temple was torn from the top to the bottom by the hand of God, creating a new and open means of access to God for all men. The means of atonement had been made. Again, God declared, "When I see the blood, I will pass over you." All men could now come boldly before the throne of God, bearing the blood of the Passover Lamb, the Messiah himself. This freedom was of far greater consequence than that at the Red Sea: this was a freedom from the bondage of sin, a release that brought abundant life and the promise of eternal life.

Again, as it was in Egypt, it was some time before the final liberation was achieved. The sacrifice of the lamb secured the downpayment on freedom, but the Red Sea crossing was required for the total liberty that was fully realized when Israel came to Sinai and entered into a covenant to become God's nation of priests. Likewise, the price for eternal freedom was paid as the blood of the Lamb spilled from the cross on Golgotha's hill; however, it was three days later when the Son of God came forth from his entombment, triumphant over death, hell, and the grave. Having crossed over the chasm between the dead and the living, he ascended into the presence of God in heaven. The death, burial, and resurrection that was prefigured in Israel's Red Sea immersion forever provided the way to freedom from sin and access to eternal life for all who would believe and apply the Lamb's blood to the doorposts and lintels of their hearts.

Though in history a few people had been resurrected from the grave by words of faith from prophets of God, never had one risen of his own accord. "I have the power to lay my life down and to take it up again," Jesus had said (John 10:17), for "I am the resurrection and the life" (John 11:25). When the massive stone was rolled away and Jesus came forth, he demonstrated his power over sin and death. In his own life, he fully conquered the last enemy that will finally be subdued for all men at the end of the age. The miracle of Passover had just taken on new and more profound proportions for the Jewish disciples of the Savior. They were commissioned to share the good news of God's new Passover provision with the entire world and to make disciples of all nations.

For those earliest Christians, Passover observance took on new meaning each year. As it had always been for them, Passover continued to be a celebration of God's deliverance from Egyptian bondage. As Jews, they were required by the terms of their covenant to remember the Passover as a memorial of God's deliverance of their ancestors from Egypt; however, Passover now took on even more profound significance, for it also became a time for celebrating the finished work of Calvary, the death of the spotless Lamb who had secured for them both freedom from sin and the gift of eternal life.

Even when these earliest Christians followed their Lord's command and took the good news to the Gentiles, the new initiates into the faith of Jesus were instructed to observe the Passover. The apostle who was officially designated as the church's ambassador to the Gentiles, Rabbi Paul, a student of Gamaliel, recommended to the Gentiles in Corinth, "Because Christ our Passover is sacrificed for us, therefore let us observe the festival . . . with the unleavened bread of sincerity and truth" (1 Corinthians 5:8). He continued to underscore the new covenant observance for Passover: "For I received from the Lord that which I also delivered to you: that the Lord Jesus on the same night in which he was betrayed took bread; and when he had given thanks, he broke it and said, 'Take, eat; this is my body which is broken for you; do this in remembrance of me.' In the same manner he also took the cup after supper, saying, 'This cup is the new covenant in my blood. This do, as often as you drink it, in remembrance of me.' For as often as you eat this bread and drink this cup, you proclaim the Lord's death till he comes" (1 Corinthians 11:23-26). Indeed, only in the context of the Passover is it possible to understand the statements that Jesus made to his disciples when he said, "Unless you eat the flesh of the Son of Man and drink his blood, you have no life in you. Whoever eats my flesh and drinks my blood has eternal life, and I will raise them up at the last day. For my flesh is real food and my blood is real drink" (John 6:63-65).

For the Christian believers, the unleavened bread of the Passover spoke of their liberation from sin and false teaching, including the "leaven" of many in the then contemporary religious establishment, which included greed (Matthew 23:14), intolerance (Matthew 23:29-33), ostentatious hypocrisy (Matthew 23:25-28), misdirected fervor (Matthew 23:15), and skepticism (Matthew 22:23ff). The paradigm is clear in Hebrew where the word *chametz* ("leaven") means "bitterness," the result of sin and unethical conduct, while the word *matzah* ("unleavened bread") means "sweet without sourness," the result of tasting and seeing that the Lord is good (Psalm 34:8) and ingesting his sweeter-than-honey divine Word (Psalm 119:103). Believers in the Messiah had left the life of bitterness of enslavement to sin and false beliefs and, as their ancestors had eaten all of the paschal lamb, they had embraced a life of consuming the Lamb of God by conforming themselves to the image of God's dear Son.

Apostolic Observance

When the time came for the first Passover following Jesus' ascension, the growing band of Jewish believers assembled in their homes to fulfill the biblical commandment regarding remembrance of the Passover. This time, however, they added to the traditional *Seder* that the sages had outlined for Passover the new order which Jesus had commissioned in remembrance of him. In effect, they celebrated two historical Passovers, the first of which secured their freedom from Egyptian bondage through the blood of the paschal lamb and the second of which liberated them from sin through the shed blood of the Passover Lamb himself. Both events were remembered just as God had commanded their remembrance in the Torah and in the words of Jesus their Lord.

This order continued in an unbroken chain of remembrance in all the Jewish households of the Christian church. Then, when the church opened the doors of faith to the Gentile nations on the basis of simple faith in the atonement of Jesus, its Jewish leaders continued their observance of the Torah as it had been expanded and completed by the teaching and example of Jesus, the Messiah. Their expanded and renewed faith represented a reformation of restoration (Hebrews 9:10), a return to the Torah's original intent of inculcating a life of lovingkindness rather than the superficial punctilious observance of commandments that characterized many in their day. A prominent feature of this reformed faith was the annual observance of

Passover which honored two acts of divine deliverance: the Exodus and Calvary.

A CONTINUING HISTORY OF OBSERVANCE

The celebration of Passover on the fourteenth day of the month Nisan, according to the Jewish calendar, continued in the early church for more than three centuries after the time of Christ. Christians celebrated what God had called "the Lord's Passover" (Exodus 12:11), and they did so on the fourteenth day of the first month of the Jewish religious calendar as "the Lord" had commanded in Leviticus 23:5: "In the first month, on the fourteenth day of the month at twilight is the LORD'S Passover." In the early second century AD, Polycarp, bishop of Smyrna, strongly defended this practice as an authentic manifestation of apostolic tradition in debates he had with Anicetus, bishop of Rome. Polycarp strongly denounced any departure from what he knew from personal experience and from the theological tradition that he had received from his mentor, the Apostle John.

Around 150 AD, the Ethiopic version of the Epistle of the Apostles declared, "And you therefore celebrate the remembrance of my death [the Passover]; then will one of you . . . be thrown into prison, and he will be grieved and sorrowful, for while you celebrate the Passover he who is in custody did not celebrate it with you." Then in 170 AD, Apollinaris, bishop of Hierapolis declared unequivocally: "The fourteenth of Nisan is the true Passover of the Lord, the great Sacrifice; instead of the lamb we have the Son of God . . . who was buried on the day of the Passover."

In the third century, as Judaeophobia and Antisemitism came to characterize official Christianity, the position that Christians should not connect the foundational event of

Christian piety with Judaism and the Jewish people gained more and more proponents. During this time, the church engaged in a wide-ranging debate that came to be called the "Quartodeciman Controversy" meaning the "Fourteener Controversy," a reference to the celebration of the death of Jesus on the fourteenth day of Nisan on the Jewish calendar. This conflict reflected a growing trend that was focused primarily in Western Christianity against fixing the date for celebrating the resurrection of Jesus by consulting with the Jewish calendar (rather than the Julian calendar) and by associating it directly with Passover. Those who had faithfully celebrated the death of Jesus and his resurrection at the time of Passover and the Festival of Firstfruits according to the Jewish calendar were pejoratively labeled "Quartodecimans" (literally "Fourteeners") by those who opposed them.

The "Quartodecimans" stood on the solid ground in their continued Christian observance of Passover. Citing Polycarp's arguments that all of the apostles observed the Passover because Scripture required it and that the apostles had instructed him in the proper method of Passover observance, these "Quartodecimans" stood on the solid authority of the Hebrew Scriptures (commonly called the "Old Testament") and the Apostolic Scriptures (commonly called the "New Testament"), as well as on the tradition of both the apostles and the second-century Apostolic Fathers. The fact that they were pejoratively caricatured as "Fourteeners" made it clear that they also insisted on following the biblical dating of their Passover celebrations by scheduling them on the fourteenth day of Nisan according to the Jewish calendar. Ironically, those who stood on Scripture were overwhelmed by those who recognized church tradition as more authoritative than Scripture, refusing to fulfill the commandments of both God and Jesus by remembering and memorializing the very day when redemption occurred—the day of Passover.

CHANGING DAYS AND SEASONS

As the church became increasingly Gentile in leadership and demographics, the shift away from what by then was considered "Jewish" practices was accelerated. For the Western Church, this replacement of the Jewish foundations of the Christian faith reached a point of culmination in the time of the Roman Emperor Constantine. During the Council of Nicaea in 325 AD, Constantine demanded that the church no longer have anything in common with the Jews. With his insistence, church leaders changed the time of celebration of Passover from Nisan 14 on the Jewish calendar to the first Sunday after the full moon after the vernal equinox on the Julian calendar—provided that Sunday did not fall on Passover (in which case it was moved a week away). Ironically, then, the Passover on the Jewish calendar continued to impact church doctrine and polity!

As the fourth century dawned, the growing Antisemitism of official Christianity further fanned the flame of the passionate debate that condemned connecting the pivotal events of Christianity with the Jews. Finally, the issue was taken in hand by Constantine himself who, after the Nicene Council in 325 AD had concluded, wrote a missive to those leaders who were not present for the council in which he insisted that the church should "have nothing more in common the detestable Jewish crowd; for we have received from our Saviour a different way" (Eusebius, *Life of Constantine,* vol. III, chap. XVIII. Also "Life of Constantine," *Catholic Encylcopedia*, p. 523).

The prevailing attitude of hostility toward the Jews that

precipitated this tragic departure from apostolic Christianity is confirmed in Theodoret's more detailed account of Constantine's letter: "It was, in the first place, declared improper to follow the custom of the Jews in the celebration of his holy festival, because, their hands having been stained with crime, the minds of these wretched men are necessarily blinded. . . . Let us, then, have nothing in common with the Jews, who are our adversaries . . . studiously avoiding all contact with that evil way . . . for how can they entertain right views on any point . . . being out of their minds, [they] are guided not by sound reason, but by an unrestrained passion, wherever their innate madness carries them . . . lest your pure minds should appear to share in the customs of a people so utterly depraved. . . . Therefore, this irregularity [Passover observance on the fourteenth day of Nisan] must be corrected, in order that we may no more have anything in common with those parricides and the murderers of our Lord" (Theodoret, *Ecclesiastical History*, Book 1, chapter 9).

Even after the practice of Passover observance had been curtailed in the Western Church, Epiphanius (circa 315-403 A.D.) continued to report the fact that earlier church leaders had insisted that Passover be observed each year on Nisan 14, saying, "You shall not change the calculation of the time, but you shall celebrate it at the same time as your brethren who came out from the circumcision. With them observe the Passover."

The Eastern (Orthodox) Church continued to observe Passover on Nisan 14 until the eleventh century, refusing to follow their Western counterparts into this error. After that time, a few Christians through the centuries remained faithful to the idea of remembering the death of Jesus on the very day on which he gave his life for man's salvation, the day of Passover; however, they were in a profoundly insignificant minority. The vast majority of the church has followed blindly in the error initiated by anti-Jewish zealots and supersessionists beginning in the third century.

After the eleventh century, Passover observance vanished from official Christian tradition and experience. The church's emphasis shifted from focusing on the celebration of Christ's death to honoring his resurrection. In time, this celebration came to be connected with Germanic, Nordic, and Anglo-Saxon spring festivals. The word *Easter* was adopted as a name for the Sunday on which the Western churches chose to celebrate the resurrection. This term is from the Old English word *Eastre* or *Eostre* that dates from the ninth century AD and is connected with *Eostre*, the Anglo-Saxon goddess of Spring and light (*The Barnhart Concise Dictionary of Egymology,* HarperCollins, 1995). In order to superimpose Christianity over the paganism of the European world and, in effect, supersede or coopt that system, the church associated the resurrection of Jesus with a purely polytheistic pagan celebration of the advent of Spring.

WE'VE BEEN ROBBED

This action merely continued a long tradition of crossing the lines between proper contexutalization of biblical faith and perverted syncretism with the religious practices of non-biblical cultures. In effect, it further separated the biblical events of the death, burial, and resurrection of Jesus from the original matrix in which they had occurred. What a profound tragedy! The church inflicted significant loss of its own self-identity upon millions of subsequent Christians around the world and across centuries of time when it systematically distanced itself from Judaism and the

Jewish people and, in so doing, separated itself from the Scriptures and distanced itself from the God of Scripture. The richness of the Christian heritage in biblical and second-temple Judaism was replaced by traditions from cultures whose practices the God of the Hebrew Scriptures had resoundingly condemned—and still does!

This irony continues to be perpetuated to this day as countless Christian communions insist that believers have nothing to do with the Jewish practices in which Jesus and the apostles clearly engaged throughout their lives. Much of official Christianity still has disregard, even disdain, for the obvious historical and theological connection between the Passover and the death of Jesus as well as for other Christian practices that are clearly rooted in Judaism. Believers who dare to connect the foundational events and experiences of Christian faith with what is recorded in the Hebrew Scriptures and was practiced by Jesus and the apostles are summarily denounced and shunned as "Judaizers" or "legalists" who are charged with practicing "Galatianism." It is as though many Christian leaders feel more comfortable with the likes of Plato and Aristotle and Anglo-Saxon pagans than they do with the Hebrew prophets, sages, and apostles of the Bible. The truth is that every authentic Christian fruit has a Jewish root! And everyone who wants to be a radical follower of Christ should return to the Jewish roots of his faith.

FOUNDATIONAL EVENTS

Whether official Christianity likes it or not, the day of Passover, the fourteenth day of Nisan, the first month of the Jewish calendar, has forever been established by God as foundational both to Judaism and to Christianity. In the case of both faith communities, Passover speaks of freedom and liberation from oppression. It speaks of the grace of forgiveness that God extended to his people because of the their acts of faith. It was his people's faith that provided the means by which the demands for divine justice are met and thereby made it possible for God to pass over their sins and deliver them from slavery.

The Israelites' faith was demonstrated in the sacrifice of the paschal lamb and the application of its blood to the doorposts and lintels of their houses. That faith freed them from Egyptian slavery. The Christian's faith is demonstrated in his faith that the blood shed by the Paschal Lamb of God on the cross of Calvary is forever efficacious to atone for the sins of the whole world, for those who believe on the Lord Jesus Christ unto eternal life (John 1:29). This faith delivers all believers from the bondage of sin and death into the glorious liberty of the children of God (Romans 8:21).

Because of the momentous events of the day of Passover, both Jews and Christians are called to remember God's mighty acts and to celebrate his goodness throughout all their generations (Exodus 12:14; Leviticus 23:14, 21, 31, 41) even to the end of the age when the Messiah himself will once again commemorate the Lord's Passover in his kingdom (Matthew 26:29).

Then, both God and humankind will celebrate God's victory over death through his Son Jesus Christ.

More Like Jesus

If Jesus celebrated the Passover every year of his life on earth and if he is going to celebrate it anew in the kingdom to come, is there any legitimate reason why any Christian would not want to follow his Lord's example in carrying out this remembrance in the present age? Indeed, Paul simply echoed Jesus' words when he urged the Corinthian believers, "Therefore, let us observe the festival with the unleavened bread of sincerity and truth, for Christ, our Passover lamb, has been sacrificed" (1 Corinthians 5:7, NIV). And he also merely followed in the footsteps of John the Baptizer, who, when he saw the approaching Jesus, exclaimed, "Behold the Lamb of God who takes away the sin of the world" (John 1:29).

It is altogether appropriate for Christians to join with the Jewish community in celebrating God's deliverance of the Israelites from Egyptian slavery. This significant event in salvation history was foundational not only to Judaism but also to Christianity. Without the Exodus, God's promise to Abraham that his descendants would inherit the land of Israel—and would do so after a sojourn in Egypt for more than 400 years—would have failed, and the faith of Abraham on which Christianity rests would have proven false as well (Romans 4:12). Secondarily, the Passover was the event that liberated all the Israelites, but it was also the event that made it possible for the Messiah to be born in Bethlehem in fulfillment of the prophecy of Micah 5:2. Because it was a faith event that fulfilled God's promises and prepared for the coming of the Messiah, Passover is just as important to Christians as it is to the Jewish people—

and perhaps more so. Without the first Passover, the first New Covenant Passover might never have occurred.

In truth, there is never a reason why Christians should not celebrate liberty and freedom from slavery. This is one of the most sacred of all biblical premises. No human being should be the victim of another by being held in captivity against his will. If God does not enslave people and has never done so, human beings certainly have no right to do so. Celebrating human freedom by joining the Jewish people in honoring the Passover within the context of the order that they established for doing so is, therefore, honorable for Christians.

At the same time, joining with Jesus, the apostles, and the Apostolic Fathers in honoring the day of Passover as a time for celebrating both the Israelite exodus from Egypt and the death, burial, and resurrection of Jesus is an act of reverence for the God who created and ordered both events. It is yet another remembrance device that helps keep Christians diligent in faithfulness to God and his Word, believing and doing all things that the Father has said. It fulfills the reason for God's commandment that the Passover be observed: "Remember this day, in which you came out from Egypt, out of the house of bondage" (Exodus 13:3), and it fulfills the reason for Jesus' commandment that his disciples observe Passover: "This do in remembrance of me" (Luke 22:19).

In view of the overwhelming scriptural evidence for the right—and even responsibility—of Christians to follow the instructions of God and of Christ, why would any Christian not want to experience the joy of celebrating the Passover with the Jewish people of history and with Jesus and the apostles in the communion of saints? The choice is yours. Do you have to? No! Do you get to? Yes!

Chapter 3

Passover: Sacrifice and Baptism

The physical liberation that ancient Israel experienced on the very first Passover through the outstretched arm of Yahweh, their God, was not an end in itself. It was only the beginning, the corporeal freedom that made possible their pilgrimage to spiritual redemption. Every observant Jew since the time of the Exodus from Egyptian bondage has affirmed the fact that man's freedom does not consist in physical liberation alone because immediately after remembering Passover as the day of deliverance, he begins the countdown toward Pentecost and spiritual redemption. This is the time of the counting of the *omer*, the seven weeks and one day from which we get the term *Pentecost* (fiftieth). The specific reason that God gave to Moses for commanding Pharaoh, "Let my people go!" was "so that they may worship" their God (Exodus 5:1). Indeed, the text actually describes God's reason thus: "so that they may celebrate a festival unto me in the desert." Without the fifty days that followed that first Passover, Israel's deliverance would have been meaningless, for without the giving of the Torah at Sinai on the day of Pentecost, the Exodus would never have been complete. Israel would still have been in bondage.

The first fifty days of Israel's journey toward the Promised Land were filled with miracles that confirmed God's will for his people to come to worship him and receive his Torah. Foremost among these was the Red Sea event. With impassable waters in front of them and Pharaoh's armies behind them, Israel stood on the brink of annihilation. They had just been delivered from bondage when, after the tenth plague in which his own firstborn son had died, Pharaoh had relented and commanded them to leave Egypt. But Pharaoh had second thoughts and initiated hot pursuit of his slaves, and he caught up with them at the shores of the Red Sea.

In the midst of the swirling emotions of impending doom, Moses relayed God's simple word to his people: "Stand still and see the salvation of the LORD" (Exodus 14:13). An east wind then parted the waters of the Red Sea, inviting the children of Israel to use a newly opened highway of public access to safety. Then God commanded Moses: "Tell the Israelites to move on" (Exodus 14:15, NIV). At this divine word, six hundred thousand men, plus women and children, began the march between walls of water, in what must have been a terrifying challenge to their faith.

Each Israelite was required to muster from within himself a profound level of faith in God and in his prophet. They had applied the blood of the paschal lamb to the doorposts and lintels of their houses because Moses had instructed them to do so. They had left Egypt because Pharaoh had commanded it and because they were thirsty for freedom. But they walked into the Sea because they *chose* to believe that God would save them from the turbid waters that towered above their heads. The extensive and powerful nature of their faith is underscored by the fact that, shortly after the last Israelite passed between the waters, Pharaoh's entire army drowned in the same place where the Israelites had just crossed unharmed! The Israelites, therefore, had engaged by faith in a life-or-death experience, and their faith had been rewarded by complete deliverance. On the east side of the Red Sea, they danced in victory and sang, "The LORD is my strength and song, and he has become my salvation" (Exodus 15:2) for they knew that their faith had produced a mighty miracle.

Israel's Corporate Baptism

In 1 Corinthians 10:1-4, the apostle Paul compares the Israelites' Red Sea crossing with baptism, underscoring the fact that it and Israel's subsequent actions were spiritual events. "Our fathers were under the cloud, and all passed through the sea; and were all baptized unto Moses in the cloud and in the sea; and did all eat the same spiritual meat; and did all drink the same spiritual drink: for they drank of that spiritual Rock that followed them: and that Rock was Christ." According to Paul, all of Israel was baptized in the Red Sea, and all of Israel drank spiritually from Jesus, the Rock. What a profound statement, pregnant with meaning!

First Israel was physically delivered from bondage when Yahweh "passed over" them because he saw the blood circling the doors of their houses. Then, they were baptized in the Red Sea in what was both a physical and spiritual exercise. All of Israel that had just escaped death at Pharaoh's hand now experienced a death, burial, and resurrection in the Red Sea. When they walked down the slopes into the sea's bottom, they surrendered their lives to the authority and will of God. They died to self. Then, they were buried for a time between the walls of water. Finally, they were resurrected to a new life of freedom from Pharaoh's pursuing armies when they climbed up the eastern shore of the Red Sea. Their lives were no longer their own; they had surrendered them to the pleasure of God and had received them again as his gift of life and freedom.

The timing of the Red Sea event coincided with what would later become the Festival of Unleavened Bread. Could it be that God was using this exercise to remove the leaven of Egypt from the lives of the Israelites just as he was physically removing them from Egypt? It could well be that the Red Sea crossing even occurred at the time of what would later be the Festival of Firstfruits. What better metaphor could God have chosen than to reveal the coming death, burial, and resurrection of Jesus Christ, the firstfruits of the resurrection (I Corinthians 15:20, 23), in the figurative death, burial, and resurrection of Israel in the Red Sea?

In a very real sense, Israel had been reborn. Now, they were ready to journey to the mountain of God, where they would enter into a covenant to become God's bride. When Yahweh thundered from Sinai, Israel that had been reborn in the waters of Red Sea baptism responded to his commandments: "We will do, and we will hear [understand]" (Deuteronomy 5:27). The moment they agreed to accept and do God's Torah, their Passover experience was complete, they were delivered from spiritual bondage to sin and death, and they were liberated into the joy of God's children and his covenanted bride.

For the first time since Adam and Eve in the garden,

humanity had been offered the choice of life or death, blessing or cursing (Deuteronomy 30:19). Whereas before that time sin and death reigned over all men (Romans 5:14), now some could choose to live by drinking the waters from the physical rock in the desert (Exodus 17:6) and by drinking spiritually unto life eternal of the living Rock that followed them in the wilderness (1 Corinthians 10:4).

THE CONCEPT OF BAPTISM

The concept of baptism is encapsulated in the word *immersion*. To be baptized is to be immersed into something, whether it be in repentance, in sanctification, in the Holy Spirit, in the body of Messiah, in suffering, in death, or in water. In whatever form it is manifest, baptism represents complete surrender to God, to his will and to his Word.

We understand the truth of this concept when we recall that a long-standing Jewish immersion tradition was the antecedent to Christian baptism and became a paradigm for the public initiation of believers into the Christian faith. John the Baptizer did not simply have a heat stroke in the Judaean desert and suddenly invent the idea of water baptism from whole cloth! He—as well as the Messianic believers after him—was continuing a time-honored Jewish tradition. Just as Israel had been delivered from Egypt by the blood of the paschal lamb, so Gentiles who became proslytes to Judaism were initiated into Jewish faith by circumcision. Just as Israel had been baptized in the Red Sea, so proselytes were required to be immersed in the waters of Israel's *mikvot* (ritual immersion pools filled with "living water" either from a flowing stream or from rain). Then, just as Israel had come before Sinai to receive God's law, converted believers were taught the same Torah.

Not only Gentile proselytes submitted themselves to the waters of the *mikveh*. The Jewish people did so as well when they experienced any ceremonial uncleanness, they immersed themselves in the water, not to cleanse themselves physically, but to demonstrate their submission to the washing of God's Word. The installation of high priests and the inauguration of kings featured immersion to confirm that they had experienced a forensic change into a new state of existence.

Many teachers among the Jews had come to characterize the *mikveh* experience as a "death, burial, and resurrection." Some had even considered it an opportunity to reenter the waters of the womb and be reborn. Paul's use of these metaphors is more clearly understood when they are returned to the Hebrew matrix from which they came. Believers in Messiah Jesus were considered to have been immersed in his death, buried with him in baptism so that they could be raised in a newness of life (Romans 6:3-5). They were born again (from above) in the metaphor that Nicodemus, the Jewish rabbi, could not understand even though the term *born again* had applied to proselytes' being born again when they accepted the Torah, were circumcised, and then were immersed in the waters of the *mikveh*. The Jewish leader simply did not know how to relate to Jesus' new application of that tradition (John 3:3, 5).

Following Jesus' example, those who came to faith in the Messiah were all immersed in the waters of *mikveh* to demonstrate their obedience to Christ in life and death. They experienced a death, burial, and resurrection similar in nature to what Jesus himself experienced on the cross, in the tomb, and in the resurrection. Their initiatory baptismal rite, like that of their Israelite ancestors, was not for physical uncleanness, but for the answer of a good conscience before God (1 Peter 3:21). Anyone who had not repented from sins only entered the water a dry sinner and came out a wet sinner! Water baptism was efficacious only if the heart hd been immersed in the Godly sorrow of repentance (2 Corinthians 7:10). It was the baptism into repentence that was the baptism into Christ which freed the believer from sin and death, just as the Israelites had been delivered from slavery and death by passing through the waters of the Red Sea.

BAPTISM AND REPENTANCE

When John came baptizing in Jordan, both the exercise and its location had profound significance. The Baptist was telling all of Israel that they, like Gentile proselytes, needed to immerse themselves first in repentance and then in water. He brought them to the Jordan at the same place where their forefathers, the second generation after the Red Sea experience, had crossed the Jordan River on dry land to enter the Promised Land and, in so doing, had also shared the same death, burial, and resurrection that their parents had experienced in the Red Sea crossing.

There at the same ford where the Jordan River had parted when the priests had dutifully carried the Ark of the Covenant from the wilderness into the land of milk and honey, John urged his fellow Jews to turn their backs on the land of Israel, reenter the water, and then turn in true repentance, thereby renewing their covenant with Yahweh. This physical action graphically demonstrated the image of the Hebrew word for the repentance, *teshuvah* (meaning "to turn"). This was the kind of repentance that John required of his fellow Jews before he would allow them to be baptized (Matthew 3:7-8).

A physical act of turning around spiritually, immersing themselves in water, and then turning around physically demonstrated what was occurring in their hearts. These Israelites were receiving the opportunity to accept the kingdom of God, welcoming Yahweh's dominion in their lives and preparing for the coming of their Messiah. It was in one of these events that Jesus came to be baptized of John and was welcomed by the Baptizer's exclamation of joy: "Behold the Lamb of God who takes away the sin of the world" (John 1:29). The new Moses whom Israel was to hear and obey (Acts 3:22) had appeared on the scene of human suffering to bring total deliverance from the power of sin (Romans 6:22) and to give to all who believe the gift of eternal life (John 3:16).

CHRISTIAN PASSOVER AND BAPTISM

Christians are empowered by God's grace to allow faith to be produced in their hearts (Ephesians 2:8) as they hear the word of the gospel (Romans 10:17). The moment they do, they eat of the Lamb that was sacrificed on the day of Passover (1 Corinthians 5:7; John 6:53), and in that act of faith, they are set free. God passes over their sins, accepting their faith and, in return, imputes to them the righteousness of Jesus Christ (Romans 4:22-24). Then, being freely justified by his grace, believers in Messiah have peace with God (Romans 5:1).

A new believer in Christ experiences the reality of what Israel's experiences foreshadowed. His Passover is not just a day of memorial—it is a person: Christ our Passover. His *Shabbat* is not merely a rest day—it is a person: Jesus, the Lord of the Sabbath. His *mikveh* is not just a pool of water for ceremonial ablutions—it is the washing of the water by the Word of God (Ephesians 5:26) in which the truth sanctifies and cleanses the heart of the believer and draws him inexorably closer to God (John 17:17). He receives not a law engraved by the finger of God on stone tablets—he receives the indwelling Lawgiver, himself, the Holy Spirit. He does not become Jewish merely through physical ancestry—he becomes Jewish in spirit when his heart experiences the circumcision which Moses and the prophet Jeremiah envisioned (Deuteronomy 10:16; 30:6; Jeremiah 4:4; Romans 2:29). He comes not to Sinai, the physical mountain that burned with fire—he joins the spiritual Zion, the heavenly Jerusalem (Hebrews 12:21, 22).

Each time a new believer is initiated into Christian faith through the baptism of repentance, he is participating in a long-standing tradition that the church inherited from Judaism. He partakes of the Passover Lamb whose blood covers and removes his sins. He partakes of the unleavened bread of sweetness that replaces the bitter leaven of his sin. Through the waters of baptism he demonstrates to the sinful world just as Israel demonstrated to Pharaoh that the God of the Bible is a deliverer, one who helps his chosen people pass from the curse of death into the promise of everlasting life by being translated from the darkness of this world into the kingdom of Messiah (Colossians 1:13). The Christian believer is dead to the world through the body of Christ (Romans 7:4), buried with him in baptism (Colossians 2:12), and raised with him to the newness of life in the Holy Spirit (Romans 6:4).

For the Christian believer, then, Passover and the events that followed it represent sacrifice and baptism, the spiritual rebirth, a death, burial, and resurrection through Christ Jesus that translates him from the kingdoms of this world into the glorious kingdom of God's dear Son (Colossians

1:13). "O the depth of the riches both of the wisdom and knowledge of God! How unsearchable are his judgments, and his ways past finding out! . . . For of him, and through him, and to him, are all things: to whom be glory for ever. Amen" (Romans 11:33-36).

Chapter 4

Passover: *Seder* and *Haggadah*

Beginning with the Exodus event, God commanded the Israelites to celebrate the Passover each year throughout all their generations (Exodus 12:24), and the Jewish people have faithfully observed the commandment without exception. Thanks to the diligence of the Jewish people over the centuries, a rather comprehensive guide to the order for celebrating Passover has been developed. First, there was a general framework for the festival observance that was transmitted generationally by oral tradition. In order to facilitate the celebration of Passover in each Jewish household, the sages of Israel developed a ceremonial order that came to be called a *Seder* ("order") that unfolds the *Haggadah* ("story") of the Passover in a very systematic and inspirational manner. Though many elements were added to this order by Jewish rabbis and scholars through the centuries, the core elements of the Passover celebration that is presently employed by international Jewry was in place before the time of Jesus and the apostles and was observed at the Last Supper and after the ascension of Jesus.

A FAMILY AFFAIR

The ceremony for observance of Passover is essentially a family affair. The design of the ceremony is to transport the Jewish person—especially the children—into the context of the very first Passover in a virtual anamnesis of the event itself. The projection of the Jewish people back in time to the events of the Passover fulfills God's commandment: "And it shall be when your son asks you in time to come, saying, What is this? then you shall say to him, With a powerful hand the LORD brought *us* out of Egypt, from the house of slavery. When Pharaoh stubbornly refused to let *us* go, the LORD killed the firstborn of both people and animals in Egypt. This is why *I* sacrifice to the LORD the first male offspring of every womb and redeem each of *my* firstborn sons" (Exodus 13:14-15, NASB emphasis added).

The sages recognized the fact that God's commandment was first an instruction for each Jewish father to teach his children in their home the truth about the foundational nature of Passover as the event of history that secured the freedom of the Israelites so that they could follow God's summons to come to Sinai and there to become his chosen nation. Secondarily, God's commandment put the language in the first person, not the third person: "The LORD brought *us* out . . . Pharaoh refused to let *us* go . . . This is why *I* sacrifice . . . and redeem each of *my* firstborn sons." God's instructions to the Israelites were profound in that they required every Jewish person to recognize that he or she was in Egypt and that he or she stood before Sinai to receive God's Law.

The Passover *Seder*, therefore, is more a teaching mechanism than it is a worship activity. It accomplishes one of the primary purposes of the Jewish family and home: educating children in the ways of God. This fulfills one of the great *mitzot* ("commandments") of the Torah: "You shall teach [my commandments] diligently to your children. Talk about them when you sit at home, and when you walk along the road, when you lie down and when you get up" (Deuteronomy 6:7, NASB, NIV).

The Passover *Seder* is, therefore, carried out in Jewish homes, not in synagogues. This fact also underscores the primacy of the home in as the center for social, educational, and religious development in the Jewish community—a lesson that Christians could learn and replicate in their own family circles. While the festivals of Judaism impact the whole community and are honored in their synagogues, the primary celebrations are in the home where they serve as means of teaching the children the time-honored traditions of the Jewish experience.

Since most Jewish people are not Torah scholars like their rabbis, they are provided with a *Haggadah*, a written form of the story of Passover which is arranged in a systematic order (*Seder*). This makes it easy for every member of a Jewish family or community to share in the remembrance of the Passover with full assurance that the order prescribed by the sages is being fulfilled.

AN ANCIENT ORDER

The Passover *Seder* that is employed in Jewish homes today is of very ancient origin. A significant portion of it certainly predates the time of the second temple. Amazingly, by the time of Jesus, much of the outline for commemoration of Passover that is used by the Jewish community today was already in place. This is readily demonstrated by the fact that in his Last Supper experience of the Passover with his disciples, Jesus employed elements of the Passover *Seder* that were not mentioned in the Hebrew Scriptures.

Jesus used at least two cups of wine as he celebrated Passover with his disciples, and he did so in the order which the *Seder* prescribed. Wine is not one of the elements required by God in his outline for the celebration of Passover: "They shall eat the flesh . . . roasted with fire, and they shall eat it with unleavened bread and bitter herbs" (Exodus 12:8; Numbers 9:11). God required, therefore, three elements for the Passover Supper: roasted lamb, unleavened bread, and bitter herbs. The use of wine at Passover is nowhere mentioned in the Hebrew Scriptures. The fact that Jesus employed the cup of wine in his last Passover celebration with his disciples is evidence first that this element had been added to the ceremony by the sages of Israel and second that Jesus himself respected and honored the practices of his people that were connected with and added to the requirements of Scripture.

The Apostolic Scriptures record Jesus' actions in the Last Supper: "After supper he took the cup, saying, This cup is the new covenant in my blood; do this, whenever you drink it, in remembrance of me" (1 Corinthians 11:25, NIV). The fact that Jesus shared a cup of wine with his disciples *after* the meal confirms that he was engaged in the *Seder* common to his Jewish family and community in that time. This confirms the fact that the cup was actually the third of four cups that were shared during the course of the *Seder* in commemoration of God's promises to the Israelites while they were in Egypt: 1) "I will bring you out from under the burdens of the Egyptians," 2) "I will deliver you from their bondage," 3) "I will also redeem you with an outstretched arm," and 4) "I will take you for my people, and I will be your God" (Exodus 6:6-7). The cup of wine was, therefore, a significant part of the ancient and continuing *Seder*.

The third of the four cups of wine employed in the traditional *Seder* came to be called "The Cup of Redemption" based on God's promise, "I will also redeem you." This cup was consumed immediately after the Passover meal of roasted lamb, *matzah* (unleavened bread), and bitter herbs had been eaten. It is clear, therefore, that Jesus continued not only the ceremony and instructions required in the Scriptures but also the *Seder* for Passover observance that had become traditional among his people. This is evidence that Jesus was in no way seeking to separate or distance himself from the Torah or the traditions of his Jewish family and community in order to start a new religion called Christianity.

This truth further validates the historicity of the Passover *Seder* as it has been celebrated by the Jewish people for at least two millennia and as it continues to be observed today. It also confirms that Christians have every right to follow their own rabbi (Jesus) in carrying out this *Seder*, especially in the way in which Jesus and the apostles did with the specific elements which the Apostolic Scriptures confirm that they employed. The reality is that Christians should be so familiar with the Jewish *Seder*, especially the one Jesus employed at the Last Supper, that they would be completely comfortable and knowledgable in sharing a traditional Passover *Seder* with their Jewish friends. This demonstrates respect for the religion that Jesus and his apostles practiced throughout their lifetimes, and it confirms every Christian's historical and theological connection with the Jewish people and their faith.

In whatever form or setting, Christians should approach the Passover *Seder* with the highest respect and honor, not just for the nuggets of insight about Jesus that they can mine from the language and symbolism of the practice but for the time-honored tradition by which the Jewish people for 3500 years have shown their respect for God's instructions by doing what he commanded. Christians should also honor the Passover in response to the reasons for which God gave it to the Israelites in the first place—as a memorial of redemption and freedom from slavery and the release of the people of God into the joys of the covenant of promise that they received at Mt. Sinai.

You will want to study the *Seder* in detail to see what God said and why he said it to his people. And you will want to see in the Passover celebration Christianity's historical and theological Jewish connection that will enrich your faith and draw you closer to God through the Messiah in the power of the Holy Spirit. When you fully understand the biblical story of Israel's deliverance from Egypt and when you are familiar with the system that the sages established for the continuing remembrance of the Passover as God had commanded, you will have a more comprehensive understanding of how Passover impacted the lives of Jesus and the apostles. This, in turn, will make your own celebration of Passover all the more meaningful and spiritually rewarding.

Chapter 5

Preparations for a Passover *Seder*

In order to have an effective celebration of Passover in your home or community, you will need to make advance preparations. You should acquire and prepare the following elements before you begin your Passover *Seder*:

For the Leader:

✡ Candlesticks and white candles, two if the day of Passover occurs on a Sabbath, otherwise one for each table.

✡ One bowl of saltwater.

✡ One shankbone of a lamb (or any roasted bone of a levitically permitted animal, symbolizing the Passover lamb). This bone should be roasted until brown.

✡ Three entire pieces of *matzah* inserted either in a *matzah* bag or between four linen napkins.

✡ One roasted egg, first boiled and then roasted in a frying pan until brown.

✡ One bowl of water with a towel.

✡ Four ornate cups, goblets, or wine glasses.
✡ Wine or grape juice.

For the Celebrants:

✡ Place settings for each participant, including plates and silverware (which can be paper and plastic if preferred).

✡ One copy of the *Haggadah* giving the order of celebration for each celebrant. This should be placed beside the place setting for easy access and ready participation.

✡ Parsley—two sprigs per person.

✡ Bitter Herbs—usually ½ teaspoon per person. Fresh horseradish is preferred. Strong horseradish also conveys the idea of the bitterness of Egypt much better than mild horseradish does.

✡ *Charoset*—at least 1 tablespoon per person. Chop apples and nuts; mix them with honey, cinnamon, and wine or grape juice.

✡ Saltwater—one small bowl of intensely salted water well-mixed (kosher salt is best) for each group of 4 to 5 people. This is to demonstrate the tears of the Jewish people, so it should be very salty.

✡ *Matzah*—enough for each person to have approximately one-fourth of a full piece of *matzah*. *Matzah* is generally sold in square pieces; however, round *matzah* is also appropriate and is probably nearer the shape of the unleavened bread that was used in Jesus' time.

✡ One cup per person. This can be a small cup or piece of stemware.

✡ Wine or grape juice adequate to fill each celebrant's cup about one-third full four times.

Chapter 6

A Christian Passover Celebration

A CHRISTIAN *HAGGADAH*

INTRODUCTION

Leader:

We are honored and grateful that we have been invited by the Eternal God of heaven and earth to celebrate the Passover that he so graciously has provided for us as families among his chosen people. Our spiritual forebears were slaves in Egypt when God Almighty with his outstretched arm delivered them and us from bondage on this very night and brought all of us unto himself to redeem us and make us a kingdom of priests. We were also slaves to sin when the Eternal Father on this very day gave the gift of his only begotten Son, Jesus Christ (*Yeshua HaMashiach*), to adopt us as his children and to deliver us from the power of the evil one.

We come to this table not necessarily because our linear ancestors were delivered from Egypt but because we have become naturalized citizens in the commonwealth of Israel through our faith in Jesus Christ, the one who brought Israel's light to the nations. Whether native born or naturalized, we are all fellow citizens in God's nation and among his chosen people, Israel.

Because the God of Abraham, Isaac, and Jacob has instructed his children to keep the Passover throughout all generations and because Jesus, our Passover, has been sacrificed for us, as a part of the nation of Israel,

Leader and People:

Therefore, let us observe the festival with the unleavened bread of sincerity and truth.

THE *HAGGADAH*

Leader:

Passover is the oldest and most important of the biblical festivals. It is foundational to God's people in that on this very day the miraculous event occurred that liberated the children of Israel from slavery and brought them to the mountain of God where they corporately joined with the Eternal to be his chosen people. Passover is also foundational to Christianity in that on this very day Jesus the Messiah (*Yeshua HaMashiach*) bore in his body on the cross of Calvary the sins of the entire world and provided the eternal sacrifice by which men of all nations are reconciled to God.

Because believers in God are commanded by him to "remember that you were slaves in Egypt," observant Jews consider that not only their ancestors, but also they themselves were enslaved in Pharaoh's onerous bondage and that they were personally delivered by the outstretched arm of God. This is the reason that the observance of Passover has been commanded by the Creator "for ever, throughout all your generations," and this is the reason we, as part of God's covenant people, observe it today.

Israel had been enslaved for over 200 years, forced into ever more difficult and torturous labor to build the splendor of Egypt. The bondage grew more severe and the taskmasters more harsh until finally the Israelites cried out to God for deliverance. God's response was to send a deliverer named Moses. In time, this Israelite prophet, who had been reared as the son of Pharaoh's daughter, came face to face with God and heard the divine voice speaking to him from a burning bush, telling him, "Go down to Egypt and tell Pharaoh, 'Let my people go.'"

With the help of his brother Aaron, Moses delivered this fateful message. The results were predictable, for even human history's greatest diplomat could not have easily secured the Israelites' release. When Pharaoh refused to hear God's command, ten plagues were poured out upon Egypt. Each plague grew in intensity until finally, the last plague was pronounced upon Egypt, a horrific event in which all the firstborn of the land were to die.

As the night of Passover approached, all Israelite families were instructed to sacrifice an unblemished lamb at the threshold of the doors to their houses. Then, the blood was applied with a bunch of hyssop to the doorposts and lintel of the house. God had said, "When I see the blood, I will pass over you." The blood encircling the doors of their houses was a public demonstration of each Israelite family's confidence in God and his word.

As God passed through Egypt, all the houses where blood was not applied suffered the loss of their firstborn.

When Pharaoh realized that his obstinacy had resulted in the widespread loss of life in Egypt, he relented and ordered the Israelites to leave Egypt.

The miraculous events of the Passover season were of such magnitude that Israel was commanded to remember God's deliverance throughout all their generations. All the Israelites were to remember that they were there, enduring the slavery, fearfully offering the paschal lamb, faithfully applying the blood to the door, triumphantly departing from Egypt, standing in trepidation at the Red Sea, marching with faith through the divided waters, watching in awe the destruction of Egypt's armies, and singing the song of triumph, saying:

People:

We, too, were there!

Leader:

Some fifteen hundred years later, as the vast majority of the world languished in bondage to sin, God expanded his covenant with Israel to include all people. The nations that had not known God were to be brought near to him and included within his chosen people by the provision of a perfect and eternal sacrifice for sin. God determined that his only begotten Son, *Yeshua HaMashiach*, would enter into the world when Mary, a virgin daughter of Israel, would be overshadowed by the Holy Spirit and would conceive the Son of Man. The entire world was to be saved as a Son of Israel was to take Israel's light to the nations.

Jesus became the doorway to eternal life in much the same manner as the doors of Israelite households became portals to life by being encircled with blood. With five wounds—in his head, his back, his hands, his feet, and his side—Jesus' entire body was likewise encircled with blood. As the Paschal Lamb, he provided the blood by which God could pass over the sins of mankind, and he became the door to eternal life.

Jesus was nailed to the cross. Six excruciating hours later when the work of redemption had been completed, he exclaimed, "It is finished," and he died. At that moment, the massive curtain in the temple was torn from the top to the bottom, as God created a new means of access into the heavenly Holy of Holies. At the same moment when thousands of his Jewish brethren were offering their family Passover lambs in the temple, the Lamb of God who came to take away the sins of the world was being offered by his Father on the cross of Calvary at Golgotha, the "Place of the Skull."

Death, however, could not hold the resurrection and the life, for three days later he arose and would ascend into Glory, to be seated at the Father's right hand, there to intercede as High Priest for all the human race. Since that time, all men everywhere have been invited to come to the foot of the cross to be reconciled to God through the atonement of the Passover Lamb. Every knee that has bowed in repentance and contrition has been raised again in the newness of life with the promise of a resurrection unto life eternal. In a very real sense, therefore, all who have accepted Jesus as Lord and Savior can say:

Leader and People:

We, too, were there!

Leader:

The struggle for freedom is continuous. In every age, there are new elements that strive for mastery over the human spirit, enslaving people anew by binding them either to human political systems or to the sinful desires of their own flesh. Each generation is obligated to continue the dynamic march toward freedom. The Hebrew word translated "freedom" is dynamic, not static. This is to say that "freedom" is an action, not a state of being. Our freedom in Christ likewise is not only a state of being but also a maximal dynamic, an ongoing series of liberating events manifest continually in our lives.

Leader:

We, therefore, see ourselves as full participants in the freedom of the Exodus as well as the liberty of Calvary, wherein Jesus' self-sacrifice as our Passover Lamb has made us free from sin and death. We, therefore, rededicate our lives to the struggle of freedom for all humankind.

THE SEDER

Leader:

The sages of Israel have provided a *seder*, an "order" which ensures that the Passover meal is properly observed. A generation before the time of Jesus, Hillel explained that only three elements were necessary for the proper observance of Passover: the lamb, unleavened bread, and bitter herbs. Other sages, however, added elements to the *Haggadah* (narrative) in its proper order.

Leader and People:

We join our hearts in celebrating this joyous festival, the Lord's Passover.

CHECKING FOR LEAVEN

(Though this exercise is not required at the Passover celebration, families and congregations may consider it profitable. If so, the leader will have hidden ten pieces of leavened bread in the home or sanctuary prior to the ceremony.)

Leader:

God's Divine Instruction, the Torah, commanded Israel to remove all leaven from their houses.

Men:

"Seven days shall you eat unleavened bread; on the first day you shall remove leaven from your houses" (Exodus 12:15).

Leader:

The Apostolic Writings agree that we must remove the leaven of sin from our lives.

Women:

"Purge out therefore the old leaven, that you may be a new lump, since you are truly unleavened" (1 Corinthians 5:7).

Leader:

Because of God's commandment that all leaven be removed from every household prior to the Passover, extensive and thorough efforts are made in every observant Jewish home to clean the entire house, particularly areas for preparing and eating food. The Western world has received this tradition as "spring cleaning."

After the house is thoroughly cleaned so that all leaven is removed, a parent intentionally hides ten pieces of leavened bread (*chametz*) in the house. In order to reinforce the importance of removing leaven from the house, the parent invites the children to search for the leaven. When they find it, however, they are not permitted to touch it. Instead, they call their parent who takes a wooden spoon and a feather and gently and thoroughly removes the leaven to be burned.

This is a great object lesson for us as children of our heavenly Father. In Jewish tradition, leaven came to represent the potential for corruption and sin. In Christian tradition, leaven represents sin and unfaithfulness to the Word and will of God. We are invited by our Father to search for even the hidden sins in our lives; however, when we discover them, we cannot deal with them ourselves. We must turn to our Father who gently and thoroughly removes them from our lives and casts them into the fire.

Leader:

Now, children, can you find the ten pieces of leaven?

(When the bread is found, the leader uses the feather and wooden spoon to collect it. It may be deposited outside the home or sanctuary.)

Leader:

The Apostolic Writings instruct us to observe the Lord's Passover worthily and in a proper manner, first by examining ourselves to see if we are in the faith. "For if we would judge ourselves," we are told, "we would not be judged" (1 Corinthians 11:31).

With David of old, we cry out to our Creator:

Leader and People:

"Cleanse me from secret faults. . . . Purge me with hyssop, and I shall be clean; wash me, and I shall be whiter than snow" (Psalm 19:12; 51:7).

Leader:

Our advocate with the Father, Jesus Christ the righteous, is faithful to cleanse us from all our sins. "Blessed is he whose transgression is forgiven, whose sin is covered" (Romans 4:7).

Leader and People:

We receive your pardon, O Father, and we rejoice in our fellowship with you through *Ruach haKodesh*, the "Holy Spirit."

Lighting the Passover Candles

Leader:

Our *Seder* begins with the lighting of the Passover candles, an honor that goes to the mother of the home. As God honored Mary to bring the Light of God into the world, so he honors the woman to kindle the festival lights. Light has always symbolized the Divine Presence manifest in ancient times in the *Shekhinah* and in the New Covenant in the *Ruach haKodesh* whose seven lamps of fire burn before the throne of God as well as in our hearts. "The people who sat in darkness have seen a great light; and upon those who sat in the region and shadow of death light has dawned" (Matthew 4:16), for " . . . a virgin shall conceive, and bear a son, and shall call his name Immanuel [God with us]" (Isaiah 7:14).

Mother or Female Leader:

We are gathered with loved ones and friends for this joyous celebration of our Lord's Passover. What we demonstrate is our fulfillment of our Lord's instruction:

People:

"You shall keep the feast of Unleavened Bread, for on this very day I brought your hosts out of the land of Egypt: therefore you shall observe this day, throughout the generations, as an ordinance for ever" (Exodus 12:17).

Mother or Female Leader:

Blessed are you, O Lord our God, King of the universe, who has preserved our lives so that we may celebrate your festival. As we kindle these festival lights, may the light of your presence enlighten us so that we may fully discern the significance of this occasion.

(The mother/female leader lights the Passover candles. In a corporate setting, one woman may light candles at each table.)

THE FIRST CUP
THE CUP OF SANCTIFICATION

(The leader will have four ornate cups, wine glasses, or goblets to demonstrate the four cups of Passover; however, individual participants will have only one cup that is partially filled four times preferably with red wine or grape juice.)

Leader:

The *Haggadah*, the Passover narrative, centers on the express fourfold promise of God to Israel. We fill our cups four times to celebrate God's full and free deliverance that brought the Israelites out of Egypt. Herein we remember our Father's words:

People:

"I am the Lord; [1] I will bring you out from under the burdens of the Egyptians [*Sanctification*], [2] I will rescue you from their bondage [*Deliverance and Judgment*], and [3] I will redeem you with an outstretched arm and with great judgments [*Redemption*]. [4] I will take you as my people, and I will be your God [*Thanksgiving and Consummation*]" (Exodus 6:6-7).

(Both the leader and the people's cups are partially filled.)

Leader: (as everyone elevates the cup)

בָּרוּךְ אַתָּה יְיָ אֱלֹהֵינוּ מֶלֶךְ הָעוֹלָם בּוֹרֵא פְּרִי הַגָּפֶן׃

Barukh atah Adonai, Eloheynu, Melekh ha'olam, borey pri hagafen.

Blessed are you, O Lord our God, King of the universe, who has created the fruit of the vine.

Leader and People:

Blessed are you, O Lord our God, King of the universe,

who has chosen us from among all people, and exalted us above all languages and has sanctified us with your commandments. With love have you given us, O Lord, our God, solemn days for joy, festivals and seasons for gladness. You have given us this day of the feast of Unleavened Bread, the season of our freedom, a holy convocation, a memorial of the departure from Egypt. You have chosen us, and sanctified us above all people, and you have caused us to inherit your holy festivals with joy and gladness. Blessed are you, O Lord our God, who sanctifies Israel and the appointed seasons.

People:

Blessed are you, O Lord our God, King of the universe, who has preserved us alive, sustained us, and brought us to enjoy this season.

Leader:

We praise you because you fulfill your promises to all your children. Whenever evil ones oppress us, your outstretched hand delivers us and brings us freedom, and we are restored. When the Evil One held us in the clutches of our own sin, you made provision for us through the shedding of the blood of your Son that we could be freed from sin and given the gift of eternal life.

People:

"I am the LORD: I will bring you out from under the burden of the Egyptians" (Exodus 6:6); "Take this, and divide it among yourselves: for I say unto you, I will not drink of the fruit of the vine, until the kingdom of God shall come" (Luke 22:17-18); "Therefore if the Son makes you free, you shall be free indeed . . . Sanctify them by your truth, your word is truth . . . and you shall know the truth, and the truth shall make you free" (John 8:36, 32).

(All drink of the first cup, the Cup of Sanctification and Freedom.)

THE GREEN VEGETABLE

Leader:

As a part of this Passover celebration, we eat of a green vegetable dipped in salt water. Partaking of the salt water reminds us of the tears that the Israelites shed as slaves in Egypt. It also helps us remember that the way of the transgressor is bitter and that our sins bring us great sorrow and pain. We also recall the salty water of the Red Sea.

Then, we vividly remember the bitter tears that our Lord Jesus shed in the Garden of Gethsemane when he considered the agonizing suffering and the awesome task of assuming to himself the sins of us all. We also recall that during his lonely ordeal of submission to the will of his Father, his sweat became as drops of blood.

Jesus was the Word of God made flesh, who came to bring abundant life to all. For this reason we eat a fresh, green spring vegetable to give us a vivid image of the life that liberates us from slavery, the life that gives us freedom from sin, and the eternal life that is the promise to all the righteous in the resurrection. By our acceptance of Jesus as Messiah and Lord, we have experienced the newness of life in him (Romans 6:4).

People:

"If anyone is in Christ, he is a new creation . . . If the Spirit of him who raised Jesus from the dead dwells in you, he who raised Christ from the dead will also give life to your mortal bodies through his Spirit who dwells in you" (2 Corinthians 5:17; Romans 8:11).

Leader: *(taking a piece of parsley or lettuce and lifting it up)*

בּרוּךְ אַתָּה יְיָ אֱלֹהֵינוּ מֶלֶךְ הָעוֹלָם בּוֹרֵא פְּרִי הָאֲדָמָה׃

Barukh atah Adonai Eloheynu, Melekh ha'olam, borey pri ha'adamah.

Blessed are You, O Lord our God, King of the universe, who creates the fruit of the earth.

(All dip the piece of parsley in salt water and eat it.)

The Breaking of Unleavened Bread

Leader:

In our *Seder* we have specially prepared unleavened bread. The Hebrew word for unleavened bread, *matzah*, means "sweet" and is distinctly contrasted with the Hebrew word for leavened bread, *chametz*, which means "bitter."

People:

"O taste and see that the Lord is good" (Psalm 34:8). "How sweet are your words to my taste, sweeter than honey to my mouth!" (Psalm 119:103).

Leader:

You will notice that in the process of baking this *matzah*, it was pierced in order to ensure that it did not rise from incipient yeast. In the baking process brown stripes are created along these pierced rows. This brings vividly to our minds the suffering of our Messiah.

People:

"He was wounded for our transgressions, he was bruised for our iniquities . . . and by his stripes we are healed" (Isaiah 53:5); ". . . they pierced my hands and my feet" (Psalm 22:16); ". . . they shall look on me whom they have pierced . . ." (Zechariah 12:10).

Leader:

The sages have prescribed that the unleavened bread,

one of the three essential elements of the Passover *Seder*, be received from three pieces of *matzah* separated in the folds of a napkin or in the three compartments of a specially designed bag. The three pieces of *matzah*, called by the sages "Unity," represent Abraham, Isaac, and Jacob as well as the three divisions of the Hebrew Scriptures: *Torah* (Law), *Nevi'im* (Prophets), and *Ketuvim* (Writings). They also represent the three levels of divine service in Israel: the Priests, the Levites, and the people of Israel.

It is also said that the three pieces of *matzah* can be traced to the three measures of flour which Abraham asked Sarah to bake when the angels visited him, according to tradition, on the eve of Passover. Abraham's instruction to Sarah to "be quick" in taking three measures of flour and making cakes parallels God's instruction on Passover that the Israelites were to eat the *matzah* in haste.

Many Christians have celebrated the Passover with three pieces of *matzah* to represent the three persons or modes of existence in the one God: Father, Son, and Holy Spirit. Furthermore, it is the middle of the three pieces of *matzah* that is broken into two pieces, symbolizing the body of Jesus that was broken for sin.

All *matzah* eaten on Passover is called *Lechem Oni*, "the Bread of Affliction." It was the bread that the Israelites ate at the time of their greatest suffering in Egypt. It also symbolizes the broken body of Jesus who was afflicted when the Father placed upon him the sins of us all.

People:

"I am the living bread which came down from heaven. If anyone eats of this bread, he will live for ever" (John 6:51). "For indeed Christ our Passover was sacrificed for us" (1 Corinthians 5:7).

Leader:

In the *Seder*, half of the middle *matzah* is wrapped in a linen napkin and hidden from view, later to be discovered and redeemed by the children. Traditionally this part of the middle *matzah* is called the *afikomin*, derived from the Greek *apókomein*, meaning "off-cut," the choice part of meat that was cut off before the Greek banquet began and was reserved to be eaten as "dessert."

People:

Our Messiah was "cut off from the land of the living; for the transgressions of my people he was stricken" (Isaiah 53:8); however, he was discovered to be alive, resurrected in a glorious body (Philippians 3:21).

Leader:

After we hide the *afikomin*, the remaining half of the middle *matzah* is returned to its place between the two whole *matzot*.

THE FOUR QUESTIONS

Leader:

The Word of God tells us that our children will ask questions. God has instructed us to tell them the story of the Passover so that they may know the Lord for themselves. It is both a sacred duty and a privilege to rehearse the miraculous acts of God in the story of Passover.

(The youngest child present, or different children, should ask these four questions. The most senior person present should answer the questions.)

Child:

"Why is this night different from all other nights?"

Elder:

The Israelites were slaves to Pharaoh in Egypt when

the Lord redeemed them with a mighty hand. If the Lord had not taken them out of Egypt, their children and grandchildren would still be slaves in Egypt. This is why it is our duty to tell the story of our Exodus from Egypt. The more one tells this story, the more praiseworthy he is.

Child:

On all other nights we eat leavened and unleavened bread; why on this night do we eat only unleavened bread?

Elder:

Because the Israelites left Egypt in haste, they did not have time for their bread to rise before they had to bake it; therefore, they ate only unleavened bread. Just as the Israelites left leaven behind them in Egypt, we also leave the sins of our old lives behind us when we enter the new life of faith in Jesus our Messiah.

Child:

On all other nights we eat any kind of vegetable; on this night why do we eat only bitter herbs?

Elder:

Eating bitter herbs helps us remember that the Israelites endured much bitterness and pain in Egypt's slavery. It also causes us to recall the suffering that Jesus endured when he was crucified on the cross for our sins.

Child:

On all other nights we are not required to dip in salt even once; why on this night do we dip twice?

Elder:

Dipping in salt water causes us to remember the tears shed by the Israelites in Egypt and the salt of the Red Sea. It also helps us recall the agony Jesus suffered in

Gethsemane as he faced the suffering on the cross.

Leader:

Narrating the Exodus story fulfills the commandment that we are to tell our children what occurred in that fateful time in Egypt.

People:

"And you shall tell your son in that day, saying, 'This is done because of what the Lord did unto me when I came forth out of Egypt' " (Exodus 13:8).

Leader: *(lifting the* seder *plate with his right hand and the* matzah *with his left hand)*

This is the bread of affliction which the Israelites ate in the land of Egypt; let all that are hungry enter and eat; and all who are in want, come and celebrate the Passover. This year we celebrate it here, but next year we hope to celebrate it in the land of Israel.

Leader:

Our Lord Jesus himself said,

People:

"The bread of God is he who comes down from heaven and gives life to the world . . . I am the bread of life. He who comes to me shall never hunger. . ." (John 6:33, 35).

Leader:

This year we celebrate the Passover as slaves to our humanity; next year as free, resurrected men we eat it anew at the Messiah's table in the Kingdom of God!

People:

"I will not drink of this fruit of the vine from now on until that day when I drink it anew with you in my Father's kingdom" (Matthew 26:29); "Blessed are those who are called to the marriage supper of the Lamb" (Revelation 19:9).

REHEARSING THE EXODUS STORY

Leader:

Once our spiritual ancestors were slaves to Pharaoh in Eygpt, but the Lord in his mercy through the Passover brought them out of that land with a mighty hand and an outstretched arm.

People:

Had God not rescued them from the hand of the destroyer, surely we and our children and our children's children would still be enslaved, deprived of freedom and dignity.

Leader:

Once we worshipped idols and were enslaved by our sins, but God in his goodness and mercy through Jesus, the Passover Lamb, forgave our transgressions and called us to be his people.

People:

Therefore, tonight is different from other nights because we have gathered to remember both God's deliverance from slavery and his deliverance from sin. We remember who we are and what God has done for us, and we rehearse for our children the story of God's deliverance at both the first Passover and at the first New Covenant Passover celebration.

Leader:

The Eternal God of heaven promised Abraham and Sarah that they would produce a great people through whom all the nations of the earth would be blessed. This promise was renewed to Isaac and again to Jacob. When the sovereignty of God made provision for preserving the household of Jacob by saving also the nation of Egypt, Joseph was delivered into Egypt and tried by the Word of the Lord. He became prime minister in Egypt and devised a plan to sustain all the people from seven years of famine. For this, he and his family were greatly honored.

Later a Pharaoh arose "who did not remember Joseph," and he enslaved the Israelites, imposing upon them backbreaking labor. He even ordered every newborn Israelite boy to be drowned in the River Nile. The Israelites knew nothing but labor, suffering, and tears.

People:

Our fathers cried out to God seeking an end to Egyptian oppression. God heard their cry and raised up Moses through miraculous intervention and in time brought him before Pharaoh to make the divine declaration:

All: "Let my people go."

Leader:

Pharaoh's heart was hardened. He heardened his heart and refused to obey God's command. Then, he only increased the suffering of our fathers. The Eternal God sent ten plagues upon Egypt so that Pharaoh might experience the power of God's judgment and then submit himself to the divine command.

It was God who delivered them. This is what he said: "On that same night I will pass through Egypt . . ."

People:

I, and not an angel.

Leader:

". . . and strike down every firstborn, both men and animals."

People:

I, and not a seraph.

Leader:

". . . and I will bring judgment on all the gods of Egypt."

People:

I, and not a messenger.

Leader:

". . . I am the LORD." (Exodus 12:12)

People:

I myself and none other.

THE TEN PLAGUES AND THE CUP OF DELIVERANCE AND JUDGMENT

(The second of four cups is now poured. Pour only a small amount, since no one will drink of this cup.)

Leader:

We now come to the time for recognizing the second cup, the Cup of Deliverance. This cup is one of joy; however, it is diminished by the fact that the Egyptians, who were also God's children, suffered because of Pharaoh's evil heart. The lives of those Egyptians were sacrificed to effect God's will. Now, as we recount the ten plagues, we spill a drop of wine from our cups for each plague to remember the judgment that comes upon men for worshipping false gods and bringing evil into the world.

*(As each plague is named, everyone uses a finger to take a drop of wine from the cup and let it drip onto a plate, symbolizing the finger of God's judgment for sin.)**

Leader:	***People:***
Dam	Blood
Leader:	***People:***
Tzfardeia	Frogs
Leader:	***People:***
Kinim	Vermin
Leader:	***People:***
Arov	Swarming Creatures
Leader:	***People:***
Dever	estilence
Leader:	***People:***
Sh'chin	Boils
Leader:	***People:***
Barad	Hail
Leader:	***People:***
Arbeh	Locusts
Leader:	***People:***
Choshech	Darkness
Leader:	***People:***
Makat B'Chorot	Slaying the First-Born

*Each of the ten plagues demonstrated God's judgment upon one of the Egyptian gods: 1) Blood: *Osiris*, the god of the Nile River; 2) Frogs: *Hekt*, the frog-headed goddess; 3) Lice: *Seb*, the earth god (the dust was turned into lice); 4) Swarming Creatures: *Scarabus*, the worshipped dung beetle; 5) Dying Cattle: *Apis*, the bull god; 6) Boils: *Neit*, the god of health; 7) Hail: *Shu*, the god of the atmopshere; 8) Locusts: *Serapia*, the god of the locusts; 9) Darkness: *Ra*, the sun god; 10) Death of Firstborn: the incarnate deities, Pharaoh and his son.

Leader:

Reeling from the effects of the final plague, Pharaoh relented and ordered the Israelites to leave Egypt. Again, Israel had been spared from the effects of this final plague by God's plan called "The Passover." The blood of a Passover lamb had been applied to the doorposts and lintels of all Israelite homes so that when God passed through Egypt requiring the lives of all firstborn, he could "pass over" the houses where he saw the blood.

People:

Thanks be to God for the provision of the Passover lamb that saved Israel from the final plague. Thanks be to God for providing the Passover Lamb, *Yeshua HaMashiach*, who takes away the sin of the world and saves us from the final second death.

Leader:

With this cup we celebrate God's deliverance that also brought judgment upon his enemies. God has delivered us from bondage to freedom, from darkness to light, from sorrow to joy.

People:

We rejoice, therefore, and praise him for his boundless grace.

(The second cup is poured out. No one drinks from it.)

THE THREE ESSENTIAL ELEMENTS

Leader:

Rabbi Gamaliel, a disciple of Hillel and teacher of Paul, insisted that "whoever does not discuss the following three things at the Passover festival has not fulfilled his duty, namely, *Pesach*, *Matzah*, and *Maror*."

Our Lord Jesus also partook of these three essentials on the night of the last Passover supper before his death. "[Jesus] said unto them, 'With fervent desire I have desired to eat this Passover [the *Pesach* lamb] with you before I suffer.'" (Luke 22:15); "And he took bread [*matzah*], gave thanks and broke it, and gave it to them, saying, 'This is my body which is given for you; do this in remembrance of me.'" (Luke 22:19); "Jesus answered, 'It is he to whom I will give a piece of bread when I have dipped it [in the *maror*].'" (John 13:26).

Leader: *(removing the shankbone from the* seder *plate and holding it up)*

The Passover sacrifice that the Israelites ate while the temple was standing signified the offering by which the Holy One passed over their houses in Egypt, as it is written:

People:

"You shall say, 'It is the Passover sacrifice of the LORD, who passed over the houses of the children of Israel in Egypt, when he struck the Egyptians, and delivered our households.' " (Exodus 12:27). ". . . every man shall take for himself . . . a lamb for a household . . . your lamb shall be without blemish, a male of the first year . . . ye shall keep it up until the fourteenth day of the same month. Then the whole assembly of the congregation of Israel shall kill it at twilight. And they shall take of some of the blood and put it on the two doorposts and on the lintel of the houses where they shall eat it. . . . And thus you shall eat it; with a belt on your waist, your sandals on your feet, and your staff in your hand. So ye shall eat it in haste: it is the LORD's Passover. . . . Now the blood shall be a sign for you on the houses where you are. And when I see the blood, I will pass over you, and the plague shall not be on you to destroy you, when I strike the land of Egypt" (Exodus 12:3, 5-7, 11, 13).

Leader:

This bone symbolizes the Passover lamb that was killed so the Israelite firstborn might live. The Jewish people no longer eat of the lamb because they have no temple; however, they still celebrate God's grace in providing life for them through the death of another.

***People*:**

We also recognize and celebrate the Lamb of God who was sacrificed once and for all to take away the sin of the world. Praised be his holy name.

Leader: *(removing the roasted egg from the* seder *plate and holding it up)*

One element that the sages added to the *Seder* is the egg, to remind the Jewish people of the responsibility they had to bring an offering while the temple was standing. As long as there is no temple, they can neither offer nor eat this offering; therefore, it is not eaten. The egg is also thought to be a symbol of new life and of the resurrection.

People: *(as the leader replaces the egg)*

Blessed are you, O Lord our God, King of the universe, who hears the cries of your oppressed people, brings them forth into freedom, and creates a people for yourself.

Leader: *(holding the remaining half of the middle* matzah*)*

The *matzah* we eat signifies that the bread lacked time to be leavened before the King of kings brought deliverance and redeemed Israel, as it is written:

People:

"And they baked unleavened cakes of the dough which they had brought out of Egypt; for it was not leavened, because they were driven out of Egypt and could not wait, nor had they prepared provisions for themselves" (Exodus 12:39).

Leader: (holding the bitter herbs, the maror*)*

The bitter herbs we eat remind us of the bitterness of slavery in Egypt. As sweet as freedom is now, we must always remember the bitterness of bondage, as it is written:

People:

"[The Egyptians] were in dread of the children of Israel . . . They made their lives bitter with hard labor in brick and mortar and with all kinds of work in the fields" (Exodus 1:12, 14).

Leader: (taking up the parsley and the bowl of salt water*)*

Tonight we dip the *karpas* in salt water, first to remind us of the tears in Egypt, and a second time, to remind us of our sins.

People:

"I am afflicted very much; Revive me, O LORD, according to your word! . . . How sweet are your words to my taste, sweeter than honey to my mouth!" (Psalm 119:107, 103).

The *Hallel*

Leader:

Having rehearsed the story of the first Passover, each of us now feels that we have been delivered from Egypt, and we celebrate our freedom. We can join with all those past and the future in offering praise to God by reading responsively one or more Psalms from Psalm 113-118, the first portion of the *Hallel*.

HANDWASHING

Leader:

Let us all now wash our hands as we set ourselves apart to partake of the Passover meal.

Leader and People:

Blessed are you, O Lord our God, King of the universe, who has set us apart by your word and has made us your people.

BLESSING GOD FOR THE BREAD

Leader:

We are now ready to observe the commandment to eat the *matzah*.

People:

For the sake of the one God, Father of all, and in his presence, may we do it in the name of all of Israel.

Leader: *(elevating all three* pieces of matzah *in his hand, with the broken piece remaining in the middle)*

בָּרוּךְ אַתָּה יְיָ אֱלֹהֵינוּ מֶלֶךְ הָעוֹלָם
הַמּוֹצִיא לֶחֶם מִן הָאָרֶץ׃

Baruch atah Adonai, Eloheynu, Melech ha'olam, ha motzi lechem min ha'aretz.

Blessed are you, O Lord our God, King of the universe, who brings forth bread from the earth.

Leader:

בָּרוּךְ אַתָּה יְיָ אֱלֹהֵינוּ מֶלֶךְ הָעוֹלָם אֲשֶׁר קִדְּשָׁנוּ
בְּמִצְוֹתָיו וְצִוָּנוּ עַל אֲכִילַת מַצָּה׃

Baruch atah Adonai, Eloheynu, Melech ha'olam, asher kidshanu b'mitzvotav v'tsivanu al achilat matzah.

Blessed are you, O Lord our God, King of the universe, who has set us apart us by your commandments and has commanded us concerning the *matzah*.

Eating the Matzah

Leader: *(holding up only the remaining half of the broken matzah)*

Now we eat the unleavened bread, the bread of haste, so called because our spiritual ancestors left Egypt in haste.

(Everyone is given a piece of the middle matzah.*)*

People:

"You shall eat unleavened bread, the bread of affliction, because you came out of the land of Egypt with great haste, so that all the days of your life you may remember the day of your departure from Egypt" (Deuteronomy 16:3).

(Everyone eats of a portion of the middle matzah.*)*

EATING THE BITTER HERBS

Leader: *(holding up the horseradish and the top* matzah*)*

Now we eat bitter herbs to remind us of the bitterness of our lives when we were slaves in Egypt.

(Everyone is given a piece of the top matzah.*)*

Leader:

We eat the bitter herbs with the top *matzah* because it was God our Father who commanded, "They are to eat . . . bitter herbs and bread made without yeast" (Exocus 12:8).

People:

"The Egyptians came to dread the Israelites and worked them ruthlessly. They made their lives bitter with hard labor in brick and mortar and with all kinds of work in the fields" (Exodus 1:12, 14).

Leader:

בָּרוּךְ אַתָּה יְיָ אֱלֹהֵינוּ מֶלֶךְ הָעוֹלָם אֲשֶׁר קִדְּשָׁנוּ
בְּמִצְוֹתָיו וְצִוָּנוּ עַל אֲכִילַת מָרוֹר:

Barukh atah Adonai, Eloheynu, Melekh ha'olam, asher kidshanu b'mitzvotav v'tzivanu al achilat maror.

Blessed are you, O Lord our God, King of the universe, who has set us apart by your commandments and commanded us concerning eating the bitter herbs.

(Everyone dips the matzah *in the bitter herbs and eats it.)*

Eating the Bitter Herbs and *Charoset* Together

Leader: *(taking the third piece of* matzah *and breaking off a large piece while each participant does the same.)*

We dip in the *maror* for the second time, only now we dip also in the *charoset* to remind us of the sweetness that God always brings to temper the bitterness of life's circumstances. The *charoset* is a mixture of fruit, nuts, and wine which symbolizes the mixture of clay and straw that the Israelites used to make bricks in Egypt. It is red to remind us of the blood of the lamb.

(Everyone dips one piece of matzah *in* maror *and another in* charoset, *places them together, and eats them as a sandwich. This is called a Hillel Sandwich after Hillel the Great, who initiated this practice a generation before the time of Jesus.)*

Eating the Meal

Leader:

Now let us share in the bounty of God's provision as we eat the Passover meal, rejoicing in our freedom.

(A full meal may be eaten.)

The Desert (Afikomin)

Leader:

Before the destruction of the temple, the roasted lamb was the last food that was consumed on Passover; however, since that time, the custom has been to eat the dessert, the *afikomin*, the half of the middle *matzah* that was hidden after the breaking. The *afikomin* substitutes for the Passover lamb.

(The children search for the hidden afikomin, *buried in a linen napkin.)*

Leader:

Now we must redeem the *afikomin.* The gift that we give is a deposit on the full price to be paid in the future. This is a wonderful paradigm for the Holy Spirit that is given to the believer as a deposit on the inheritance of eternal life (2 Corinthians 1:22; 5:5; Ephesians 1:13-14). As we redeem the hidden *afikomin*, we are reminded that our Lord Jesus Christ was resurrected from the dead, just as the ancient blessing declares, "Blessed are you, O Lord our God, King of the universe, who brings forth bread from the earth." Jesus, the bread from heaven, was indeed brought forth from the earth in the resurrection.

(The child who finds the afikomin *receives a reward.)*

Leader:

Called the Promise of the Father, this gift reminds us that God has sent us his Holy Spirit.

People:

"Behold, I send the promise of my Father upon you: but tarry in the city of Jerusalem until you are clothed upon with power from on high" (Luke 24:49).

Leader:

At the time of the Exodus, this piece of *matzah*, the *afikomin*, was called the bread of affliction. Indeed, Jesus was afflicted for our sins, but he was raised again the third day according to the Scriptures, ensuring for us eternal life. Just as Israel now eats this bread instead of the paschal lamb, when we eat this bread, we symbolically eat the flesh of the Lamb of God who removes the world's sin.

People:

"Therefore if the Son makes you free, you shall be free indeed" (John 8:36).

(Each participant is given an olive-sized piece of the afikomin.*)*

Leader:

This bread which we now receive, is it not the communion of the body of our Lord Jesus Christ which was broken for us?

People:

"We are all partakers of that one bread." (1 Corinthians 10:17).

Leader:

Take and eat, knowing that Christ has died for us, Christ is risen, and Christ is coming again.

(Everyone eats of the afikomin.*)*

Grace after the Meal

Leader:

Blessed are you, O Lord our God, King of the universe, who feeds the whole world with your goodness, with grace, with lovingkindness and tender mercy; you give food to all flesh, for your lovingkindness endures forever. Through your great goodness food has never failed us: O may it not fail us for ever and ever for your great Name's sake, since you nourish and sustain all beings, and do good unto all, and provide food for all your creatures whom you have created. Blessed are you, O Lord, who gives food unto all.

People:

Blessed are you, O Lord our God, because you gave us an heritage unto our fathers, a desirable, good, and ample land, the covenant and the Torah, and food in plenty. Blessed are you, O Lord, for the land and for the food.

Leader:

Have compassion, O Lord our God, upon Israel your

people, and upon the kingdom of the house of David your anointed: speedily magnify the glory of the Temple, and doubly comfort us. Blessed are you, O Lord, who in your compassion rebuilds Jerusalem. Amen.

People:

Blessed are you, O Lord our God, our Father, our King, who is kind and deals kindly with all; you have dealt kindly, do deal kindly, and will deal kindly with us.

Leader:

Let us inherit the day which is altogether good; and make us worthy of the days of the Messiah, and the life of the world to come.

Leader and People: He who makes peace in his high places, may he make peace for us and for all Israel, and say you all, Amen.

THE THIRD CUP
THE CUP OF REDEMPTION

Leader:

The third cup of Passover is the Cup of Redemption, so called because God said, "I will redeem you." It celebrated redemption from Egypt. It was this cup that our Lord Jesus shared with his disciples to introduce the New Covenant in his blood by which we celebrate our deliverance from sin.

Leader:

בָּרוּךְ אַתָּה יְיָ אֱלֹהֵינוּ מֶלֶךְ הָעוֹלָם בּוֹרֵא פְּרִי הַגָּפֶן:

Barukh atah, Adonai, Eloheynu, Melekh ha'olam, borey pri hagafen.

Blessed are you, O Lord our God, King of the universe, who creates the fruit of the vine.

Leader:

This cup which we now receive, is it not the blood that our Lord Jesus Christ shed because of our sins?

People:

"This is the cup of the new covenant" (1 Corinthians 11:25).

Leader:

Drink this cup knowing that God was in Christ reconciling the world to himself through the shedding of his blood.

(Everyone drinks of the Cup of Redemption.)

The Great *Hallel*

(The Great Hallel, *Psalm 136, is now read responsively. This was the "hymn" which Jesus and the disciples sang at the end of Passover.)*

The Fourth Cup
The Cup of Thanksgiving and Consummation

Leader:

We now partake of the Cup of Thanksgiving because God said to Israel, "I am the LORD; I will take you as my people, and I will be your God" (Exodus 6:7).

People:

Blessed are you, O Lord our God, King of the universe, who has adopted us as your children and given us the grace through which we call you, *Abba*, Father.

Leader:

This cup is also called the Cup of Consummation, for it is the one to which Jesus referred when he declared, "I will not drink of this fruit of the vine from now on until that day I drink it anew with you in my Father's kingdom" (Matthew 26:29). It speaks to us of the consummation of the relationship to which we have been espoused: "Blessed are those have been called to the marriage supper of the Lamb" (Revelation 19:9).

People:

". . . I have espoused you to one husband, that I may present you as a chaste virgin to Christ" (2 Corinthians 11:2). "The Spirit and the bride say, 'Come.' . . . And whosoever will, let him take of the water of life freely" (Revelation 22:17).

Leader:

This cup is also associated with and is sometimes called the Cup of Elijah, celebrated because of God's promise that he would send the prophet Elijah before the coming of the Messiah. We understand from the words of Jesus that John the Baptizer ministered in Elijah's spirit, and we believe that the same spirit is even now bringing restoration in the world, preparing for our Lord's return.

People:

"Even so come, Lord Jesus."

THE CONCLUSION

Leader:

And now may we join together in praying the prayer our Lord taught his disciples to pray by saying,

Leader and People:

"Our Father who art in heaven, hallowed be thyname. Thy kingdom come, thy will be done on earth as it is in heaven. Give us today our daily bread, and forgive us our debts, as we forgive our debtors. And lead us not into temptation, but deliver us from evil."

Leader:

"The LORD bless you and keep you. The LORD make his face shine upon you and be gracious unto you. The LORD turn his face toward you and give you peace."

"To him who loves us and has freed us from our sins by his blood, and has made us to be a kingdom of priests to serve his God and Father–to him be glory and power for ever and ever! Amen."

As we conclude this Passover, let us shout with all our Jewish brothers around the world:

Leader:

לַשָּׁנָה הַבָּאָה בִּירוּשָׁלָיִם:

L'shanah haba'ah b'Yerushalayim.

People:

"Next year in Jerusalem!"

All of the blessings in this ***Christian Passover Haggadah*** are presented in Hebrew and English in ***Passover Blessings and Songs***, an audiocassette produced in Israel by Yuval Shomron that is available from Holy Land Gifts (800.564.4659; www.ShofarTallit.com) or from Hebraic Christian Global Community (678.615.3568; www.HebraicCommunity.org).

Chapter 7

Celebrating Passover with Jesus and the Apostles

Jesus was a fully Torah-observant Jew, the only human being who ever fulfilled all the moral, ethical, and ceremonial requirements of the Law of God. Far from being a radical innovator who started a completely new religion, as much of Christian theology has imagined him to have been, Jesus was a faithful and obedient Son who readily affirmed that he kept all of his Father's commandments (John 15:10) and who honored the traditions of his Jewish family and community.

It was only natural, therefore, that one of the last things Jesus did with his disciples before his crucifixion was to celebrate the Passover. "I have eagerly desired to eat this Passover with you before I suffer," he told his followers, "for I tell you, I will not eat it again until it finds fulfillment in the kingdom of God" (Luke 22:15-16, NIV). Jesus was simply doing his duty as a faithful Jew, keeping the explicit commandment his Father had given to his ancestors on the day when the very first Passover occurred: "And this day shall be unto you for a memorial; and ye shall keep it a feast to the Lord throughout your generations; ye shall keep it a feast by an ordinance for ever" (Exodus 12:14, KJV).

When the Passover season approached, as a dutiful son of Israel, Jesus instructed Peter and John: "Go and make preparations for us to eat the Passover." He even described the advance provision that the Father had made for his final Passover celebration: "Go into the city, and a man carrying a jar of water will meet you. Follow him. Say to the owner of the house he enters, The Teacher asks: Where is my guest room, where I may eat the Passover with my disciples? He will show you a large room upstairs furnished and ready. Make the preparations for us there" (Luke 22:8, 10-12, NASB, NIV).

PREPARATION FOR PASSOVER

As Jesus had instructed them, "they made ready the Passover" by cleansing the house from leaven, securing the unblemished lamb for the sacrifice, preparing the bitter herbs, baking or acquiring the unleavened bread, and securing the fruit of the vine. One thing is certain: the disciples faithfully fulfilled these requirements to ensure that their Lord could rightly celebrate the last of his yearly Passovers.

When Jesus and his apostles assembled in the second-floor banqueting chamber, they did so with all the joy of the Passover season, celebrating the fact that they, like all their other Jewish brothers and sisters, had been delivered from Egyptian slavery by God's outstretched arm.

Weighing heavily over the assembly, however, was their Master's prediction that he would soon suffer at the hands of the the Roman authorities, the "Gentiles" he described in Matthew 20:18: "Behold, we are going up to Jerusalem; and the Son of Man will be delivered to the chief priests and scribes, and they will condemn him to death, and will hand him over to the Gentiles to be mocked and flogged and crucified" (NASB, NIV).

Order of Observance

The method of Passover observance had been given in general terms in the Torah itself; however, Israel's sages had expanded upon this outline to establish a *Seder* (order) for celebrating the festival. This was a part of the oral tradition that had been passed down from generation to generation. By the time of the Second Temple, most of the celebration that is currently practiced among the Jewish people was already in place in at least a rudimentary form. A generation before the time of Jesus, Hillel, one of Israel's greatest sages, affirmed the biblical premise that only three things were required for the proper celebration of Passover: the Passover lamb (*pesach*), the bitter herbs (*maror*), and the unleavened bread (*matzah*). This teaching was reinforced by Gamaliel, a contemporary of Jesus and Paul's teacher. Other elements of celebration had also been added to the traditional order, but these three requirements remained the core of the annual remembrance of Passover.

From evidence in the Gospel accounts, we can conclude that Jesus and his disciples celebrated the Passover during the final evening of his incarnation by following the order prescribed by the sages that was traditional to their time. Jesus' last Passover supper was not just an incidental meal or a casual occasion for introducing a totally new ceremony that would be called the "Lord's Supper" or "Communion." It was a careful exercise in the fulfillment of the divine commandment to remember the greatest work in Israelite history, a remembrance into which was injected an outline for celebrating God's greatest work in all of human history, the death of the Lamb of God who takes away the sin of the world. It was also done in conformity with the accepted norm for celebrating Passover in that day, the sages' *Seder*.

As they ate the Passvoer meal, Jesus and his disciples likely reclined around a triclinium, a somewhat u-shaped table. This was in keeping with the tradition that Passover celebrants were not slaves, who sat or stood while eating, but free men, nobles who in that time ate while reclining and leaning on one elbow.

To begin the Passover, as was the case with all Jewish celebrations, Jesus would have spoken the *Kiddush Berakhah* (blessing), thereby sanctifying the occasion. He would have raised the cup of the fruit of the vine and said, "Blessed are you, O Lord our God, King of the universe, who creates the fruit of the vine."

Jesus also participated in the ceremonial washing of hands. Later in the ceremony, he also introduced a profoundly new action that would be rich in meaning and depth for all Christians. He washed his disciples feet in the ultimate demonstration of humility and service, even assuming the most menial task of the most humble servant in that time.

During the course of the meal, Jesus took the unleavened bread (*matzah*) of the Passover meal, the first of three elements essential to Passover observance and blessed God for the bread by means of the traditional *HaMotzi*

Berakhah, saying: "Blessed are you, O Lord our God, Sovereign of the Universe, who brings forth bread from the earth." Then he gave the bread to his disciples to eat, saying, "This is my body which is given [broken] for you" (Luke 22:19; 1 Corinthians 11:24). In effect, by partaking of this bread, the disciples were "eating the flesh" of the Son of God as he had instructed them in John 6:53-55.

It is also very significant that Jesus shared the *matzah* with his disciples *during* the meal, not after it. In this action, he conformed his celebration of the Passover—including its new covenant application—to the tradition of the Jewish people at the time wherein it was understood that after the lamb had been eaten, no additional food was to be consumed. Jesus, the unleavened bread of sincerity and truth, was the first and the last.

It should also be noted that, in conformity with the biblical tradition, Jesus blessed God for the elements of the Passover. He did not "bless" the bread or the fruit of the vine as is commonly believed in many Christian circles. Neither the bread nor the wine required blessing in order to be "sanctified" for sacred use. They were already inherently "good" because God had made them good as part of his creation which in the beginning of time he had declared to be "very good" (Genesis 1:31).

The idea that material things need to be "blessed" or "sanctified" in order to become "holy" for sacred use is a corollary of the dualistic theme of Greek philosophy, including neo-Platonism and Gnosticism, wherein everything material was considered to be inherently evil. This, of course, does not conform with the biblical concept that everything material is "good" because God created it as such, a fact that Paul confirms in Romans 14:14: "I know and am convinced in the Lord Jesus that nothing is unclean in itself." In the record of the Gospels, Jesus simply took bread and blessed (gave thanks) and then broke it and gave it to the disciples. The word *it* is interpolated into the text by the translators under the influence of Church tradition that asserts that the elements of communion must be "blessed" by a priest or minister. The word *it* is not in the original text itself. Jesus, therefore, did precisely as his Jewish ancestors and contemporaries did. He blessed God, not the bread or the fruit of the vine.

After breaking and distributing the bread, Jesus also shared the second of the three elements essential to the celebration of Passover: the bitter herbs. He did this by dipping bread in the bitter herbs in the company of Judas, demonstrating the bitterness of betrayal in the house of his friends. The Master said of his betrayer, "It is the one to whom I will give this piece of bread when I have dipped it in the dish" (John 13:26). Even to this day, unleavened bread of Passover is dipped first in *maror* (bitter herbs), ten in *charoset* (a mixture of nuts, apples, and honey), and finally in a mixture of *maror* and *charoset*.

Next, Jesus and the disciples ate the roasted paschal lamb, the third element essential to the proper celebration of Passover. This was another of the things that his disciples were commissioned to prepare so their Master could eat the Passover that he had so much desired to share with them before his death. Everything was done in conformity with God's Word and with the tradition of the Jewish people.

Finally, after the meal, Jesus took the third cup, the Cup of Redemption and again blessed God, this time with the traditional *Pri Hagafen Berakhah*: "Blessed are you, O Lord our God, Sovereign of the universe, who creates the fruit of the vine." Then, Jesus enjoined his disciples to

drink of the cup, recognizing that as they did, they received the cup of the New Testament in his blood, in effect drinking the blood of the Son of God as he had also required in John 6:53-55.

Jesus gave no indication to his disciples that since he would be fulfilling the Passover by shedding his blood on the cross of Calvary, there would be no further need for them to continue to observe Passover. Indeed, he gave this injunction: ". . . this do in remembrance of me" (Luke 22:19), indicating that he was adding to the traditional Passover, not subtracting from it or eliminating all prior observance practices. Paul further encouraged even Gentile believers to observe the festival with the unleavened bread of sincerity and truth because "Christ our Passover is sacrificed for us" (1 Corinthians 5:7). He also observed that when Christians celebrate the Passover, including the remembrance which Jesus commanded, "you proclaim the Lord's death until he come" (1 Corinthians 11:26).

As further evidence that Jesus expected his disciples to continue the observance of Passover as God had commanded with the proviso that as believers in the Messiah they should thereafter add the practice of communion in remembrance of his death, Jesus assured his disciples that he himself would one day partake of the elements of Passover "with you in my Father's kingdom" (Matthew 26:29).

CELEBRATING TODAY WITH JESUS AND THE APOSTLES

Jesus and the apostles, then, celebrated at least the following elements of the traditional Passover Seder:

✡ *The* **Kiddush** (Cup of Sanctification)

✡ *The Washing of Hands*

✡ *The Breaking and Eating of Unleavened Bread* (whichJesus used to institute the bread of communion)

✡ *The Washing of the Disciples' Feet*

✡ *The Dipping and Eating of Bitter Herbs* (when Jesus, along with Judas, dipped bread in the bitter herbs)

✡ *The Eating of the Passover Lamb* (now celebrated by eating the *afikomin*)

✡ *The Cup of Redemption* (which Jesus used to institute the cup of communion)

✡ *The Singing of the* **Hallel**, the "hymn" that Jesus and the disciples sang together in Matthew 26:30. Most English translations use the word *hymn*; however, the New Jerusalem Bible is far more accurate with its translation "psalms." The Complete Jerusalem Bible is even more accurate with its rendering "*Hallel*," for these were precisely the Psalms that the disciples, like all of their fellow Israelites, were singing on the night of Passover.

It is very likely that Jesus and the apostles observed not only these but also other portions of the *Seder* that certainly predated the Christian era at the very least in embryonic form. The following outline, however, is a

Passover *Seder* that incorporates the elements which we know from the record of the Gospels that Jesus used when he observed the Passover with his disciples in the Last Supper.

Chapter 8

The Last Supper *Seder*

The Order Jesus Observed

Leader:

One of the last things that our Lord Jesus Christ did during his life on earth was to celebrate the Passover. First, he commemorated the Exodus from Egypt in the order (*seder*) that the sages of Israel prescribed. Then, he offered himself as the Passover Lamb who removes the sin of the world, thereby fulfilling Passover by filling it with new and expanded meaning. In anticipation of this fulfillment, Jesus commanded his disciples to remember his death until he returns by sharing bread and the fruit of the vine in remembrance of his broken body and his shed blood. As we share the Passover in the manner in which Jesus did at the Last Supper, let us rejoice in the eternal life that we have in our Messiah.

THE FIRST CUP: THE CUP OF SANCTIFICATION

Leader:

The Passover story (*Haggadah*) centers on the express fourfold promise of God to Israel. Herein we remember our Father's words:

People:

"I am the Lord; [1] I will bring you out from under the burdens of the Egyptians [*Sanctification*], [2] I will rescue you from their bondage [*Deliverance and Judgment*], and [3] I will redeem you with an outstretched arm and with great judgments [*Redemption*]. [4] I will take you as my people, and I will be your God [*Thanksgiving and Consummation*]" (Exodus 6:6-7).

(Both the leader and the people's cups are partially filled.)

Leader:

בָּרוּךְ אַתָּה יְיָ אֱלֹהֵינוּ מֶלֶךְ הָעוֹלָם בּוֹרֵא פְּרִי הַגָּפֶן׃

Barukh atah Adonai, Eloheynu, Melekh ha'olam, borey pri hagafen.

Blessed are you, O Lord our God, King of the universe, who has created the fruit of the vine.

Leader and People:

Blessed are you, O Lord our God, King of the universe, who has chosen us from among all people, and exalted us above all languages and has sanctified us with your commandments. With love have you given us, O Lord, our God, solemn days for joy, festivals and seasons for gladness. You have given us this day of the feast of Unleavened Bread, the season of our freedom, a holy convocation, a memorial of the departure from Egypt. You have chosen us, and sanctified us above all people, and you have caused us to inherit your holy festivals with joy and gladness. Blessed are you, O Lord our God, who sanctifies Israel and the appointed seasons.

Blessed are you, O Lord our God, King of the universe, who has preserved us alive, sustained us, and brought us to enjoy this season.

Leader:

We praise you because you fulfill your promises to all your children. Whenever evil ones oppress us, your outstretched hand delivers us and brings us freedom, and we are restored. When the Evil One held us in the clutches of our own sin, you made provision for us through the shedding of the blood of your Son that we could be freed from sin and given the gift of eternal life.

People:

"I am the LORD: I will bring you out from under the burden of the Egyptians" (Exodus 6:6); "Take this, and divide it among yourselves: for I say unto you, I will not drink of the fruit of the vine, until the kingdom of God shall come" (Luke 22:17-18); "Therefore if the Son makes you free, you shall be free indeed . . . Sanctify them by your truth, your word is truth . . . and you shall know the truth, and the truth shall make you free" (John 8:36, 32).

(Everyone drinks of the Cup of Sanctification.)

HAND WASHING

Leader:

The washing of hands is purely ceremonial and not for hygiene. It demonstrates the fact that everyone who comes before God must do so with "clean hands and a pure heart" (Psalm 24:4).

The lesson in the washing of hands is the fact that we are to be blameless before God and submitted one to another in love.

Leader:

Let us all now wash our hands as we set ourselves apart to partake of the Passover meal.

Leader and People:

Blessed are you, O Lord our God, King of the universe, who has set us apart by your word and has made us your people.

(All wash their hands in water.)

BREAKING OF *MATZAH*

Leader:

In our *Seder* we have specially prepared unleavened bread called *matzah*. The Hebrew term for unleavened bread, *matzah*, means "sweet" and is contrasted with the Hebrew word for leavened bread, *chametz*, which means "bitter."

People:

"O taste and see that the Lord is good" (Psalm 34:8). "How sweet are your words to my taste, sweeter than honey to my mouth!" (Psalm 119:103).

Leader:

You will notice that in the process of baking this *matzah*, it was pierced in order to ensure that it did not rise from incipient yeast. In the baking process brown stripes are created along these pierced rows. This brings vividly to our minds the suffering of our Messiah.

People:

"He was wounded for our transgressions, he was bruised

for our iniquities . . . and by his stripes we are healed" (Isaiah 53:5); ". . . they pierced my hands and my feet" (Psalm 22:16); ". . . they shall look on me whom they have pierced . . ." (Zechariah 12:10).

Leader:

The sages have prescribed that in partaking of the unleavened bread, one of the three essential elements of the Passover *Seder*, be received from three pieces of *matzah* separated in the folds of a napkin or in the three compartments of a specially designed bag. The three pieces of *matzah* represent Abraham, Isaac, and Jacob as well as the three divisions of the Hebrew Scriptures: *Torah* (Law), *Nevi'im* (Prophets), and *Ketuvim* (Writings). They also represent the three levels of divine service in Israel: the Priests, the Levites, and the people of Israel.

It is also said that the three pieces of *matzah* can be traced to the three measures of flour which Abraham asked Sarah to bake when the angels visited him, according to tradition, on the eve of Passover. Abraham's instruction to Sarah to "be quick" in taking three measures of flour and making cakes parallels God's instruction on Passover that the Israelites were to eat the *matzah* in haste.

Many Christians have celebrated the Passover with three pieces of *matzah* to represent the three persons or modes of existence in the one God: Father, Son, and Holy Spirit. Furthermore, it is the middle of the three pieces of *matzah* that is broken into two pieces, symbolizing the body of Jesus that was broken for sin.

All *matzah* eaten on Passover is called *Lechem Oni*, "the Bread of Affliction." It was the bread that the Israelites ate at the time of their greatest suffering in Egypt. It also symbolizes the broken body of Jesus who was afflicted when the Father placed upon him the sins of us all.

People:

"I am the living bread which came down from heaven. If anyone eats of this bread, he will live for ever" (John 6:51). "For indeed Christ our Passover was sacrificed for us" (1 Corinthians 5:7). "For he was cut off from the land of the living; for the transgressions of my people he was stricken" (Isaiah 53:8); however, he was discovered to be alive, resurrected in a glorious body (Philippians 3:21).

BLESSING GOD FOR THE BREAD

Leader:

We are now ready to observe the commandment to eat the *matzah*.

People:

For the sake of the one God, Father of all, and in his presence, may we do it in the name of all of Israel.

Leader: *(taking all three* matzot *in his hand)*

בָּרוּךְ אַתָּה יְיָ אֱלֹהֵינוּ מֶלֶךְ הָעוֹלָם
הַמּוֹצִיא לֶחֶם מִן הָאָרֶץ׃

Baruch atah Adonai, Eloheynu, Melech ha'olam, ha motzi lechem min ha'aretz.

Blessed are you, O Lord our God, King of the universe, who brings forth bread from the earth.

בָּרוּךְ אַתָּה יְיָ אֱלֹהֵינוּ מֶלֶךְ הָעוֹלָם אֲשֶׁר קִדְּשָׁנוּ
בְּמִצְוֹתָיו וְצִוָּנוּ עַל אֲכִילַת מַצָּה׃

Baruch atah Adonai, Eloheynu, Melech ha'olam, asher kidshanu b'mitzvotav v'tsivanu al achilat matzah.

Blessed are you, O Lord our God, King of the universe, who has set us apart us by your commandments and has commanded us concerning the *matzah*.

Eating the *Matzah*

(This is the Bread of Communion.)

Leader: *(holding up the middle* matzah *and breaking it)*

Now we eat the unleavened bread, the bread of haste, so called because our spiritual ancestors left Egypt in such haste that they had no time for their bread to rise.

People:

"You shall eat unleavened bread, the bread of affliction, because you came out of the land of Egypt with great haste, so that all the days of your life you may remember the day of your departure from Egypt" (Deuteronomy 16:3).

(All are given olive-sized pieces of the middle matzah.*)*

Leader:

At the time of the exodus *matzah* was called the bread of affliction. Indeed, Jesus was afflicted for our sins, but he was raised again the third day according to the Scriptures, ensuring for us eternal life. Just as Israel now eats this bread instead of the paschal lamb, when we eat this bread, we symbolically eat the flesh of the Lamb of God who takes away the sin of the world.

People:

"Therefore if the Son makes you free, you shall be free indeed" (John 8:36).

(All eat of the matzah.*)*

WASHING THE DISCIPLES' FEET

Our Lord Jesus not only washed his own hands during the Passover celebration, but as the meal was being served, he demonstrated the ultimate act of humility in washing the feet of the twelve disciples who shared that Last Passover with him. "After that he poured water into a basin, and began to wash the disciples' feet" (John 13:2-5). As we remember this demonstration of servanthood that our Lord gave on the night of his last Passover, we affirm our commitment to serve one another in love.

EATING THE BITTER HERBS

Leader: *(holding up the bitter herbs, usually horseradish and the top* matzah*)*

Now we eat bitter herbs to remind us of the bitterness of the Israelites when they were slaves in Egypt and of the bitterness that our Lord experienced when he was betrayed by one of his disciples.

People:

"The Egyptians came to dread the Israelites and worked them ruthlessly. They made their lives bitter with hard labor in brick and mortar and with all kinds of work in the fields" (Exodus 1:12-14).

"After he had said this, Jesus was troubled in spirit and testified, 'I tell you the truth, one of you is going to betray me. . . . It is the one to whom I will give this piece of bread when I have dipped it in the dish.' Then, dipping the piece of bread, he gave it to Judas Iscariot, son of Simon" (John 13:21, 26).

Leader:

בָּרוּךְ אַתָּה יְיָ אֱלֹהֵינוּ מֶלֶךְ הָעוֹלָם אֲשֶׁר קִדְּשָׁנוּ
בְּמִצְוֹתָיו וְצִוָּנוּ עַל אֲכִילַת מָרוֹר׃

Barukh atah Adonai, Eloheynu, Melekh ha'olam, asher kidshanu b'mitzvotav v'tzivanu al achilat maror.

Blessed are you, O Lord our God, King of the universe, who has set us apart by your word and commanded us concerning eating the bitter herbs.

(Everyone dips a piece of matzah *in the bitter herbs and eats it.)*

Eating the Passover Meal

(Jesus and the apostles ate the Passover meal, including the lamb. A meal may be eaten, or the middle matzah *may be substituted.)*

The Third Cup: The Cup of Redemption

(Everyone fills the cup. This is the Cup of Communion.)

Leader:

The third cup of Passover is the Cup of Redemption, so called because God said, "I will redeem you." It celebrated redemption from Egypt. It was this cup that our Lord Jesus shared with his disciples to introduce the New Covenant in his blood by which we celebrate our deliverance from sin.

Leader:

בָּרוּךְ אַתָּה יְיָ אֱלֹהֵינוּ מֶלֶךְ הָעוֹלָם בּוֹרֵא פְּרִי הַגָּפֶן:

Barukh atah, Adonai, Eloheynu, Melekh ha'olam, borey pri hagafen.

Blessed are you, O Lord our God, King of the universe, who creates the fruit of the vine.

Leader:

This cup which we now receive, is it not the blood that our Lord Jesus Christ shed because of our sins?

People:

"This is the cup of the new covenant" (1 Corinthians 11:25).

Leader:

Drink this cup knowing that God was in Christ reconciling the world to himself through the shedding of his blood.

(All drink of the Cup of Redemption.)

THE FOURTH CUP: THE CUP OF THANKSGIVING AND CONSUMMATION

(Jesus declared that he would not drink of this cup until the kingdom. We recognize it as the promise of his second coming.)

Leader:

This cup is called the Cup of Consummation, for it is the one to which Jesus referred when he declared, "I will not drink of this fruit of the vine from now on until that day I drink it anew with you in my Father's kingdom" (Matthew 26:29). It speaks to us of the consummation of the relationship to which we have been espoused, the marriage supper of the Lamb: "Blessed are those have been called to the marriage supper of the Lamb" (Revelation 19:9).

People:

". . . I have espoused you to one husband, that I may present you as a chaste virgin to Christ" (2 Corinthians 11:2). "The Spirit and the bride say, 'Come.' . . . And whosoever will, let him take of the water of life freely" (Revelation 22:17).

Leader:

This cup is also associated with and is sometimes called the Cup of Elijah, celebrated because of God's promise that he would send the prophet before the coming of the Messiah. We understand from the words of Jesus that John the Baptizer ministered in Elijah's spirit, and we believe that the same spirit is even now bringing restoration in the world, preparing for our Lord's return.

People:

"Even so come, Lord Jesus."

(Since Jesus said he would not drink of this cup until the kingdom, we reserve this cup to be drunk with him at that day.)

THE *HALLEL*

The Hallel Psalms (113-118) may be read responsively. From this collection of Psalms was selected the "hymn" which Jesus and the disciples sang as they concluded the Passover and left the Upper Room for the Garden of Gethsemane. (The Great Hallel, Psalm 136 is given here.)

Leader:

Oh, give thanks to the LORD, for *He is* good! For His mercy *endures* forever.

People:

Oh, give thanks to the God of gods! For His mercy *endures* forever.

Leader:

Oh, give thanks to the Lord of lords! For His mercy *endures* forever:

People:

To Him who alone does great wonders, For His mercy *endures* forever;

Leader:

To Him who by wisdom made the heavens, For His mercy *endures* forever;

People:

To Him who laid out the earth above the waters, For His mercy *endures* forever;

Leader:

To Him who made great lights, For His mercy *endures* forever —

People:

The sun to rule by day, For His mercy *endures* forever;

Leader:

The moon and stars to rule by night, For His mercy *endures* forever.

People:

To Him who struck Egypt in their firstborn, For His mercy *endures* forever;

Leader:

And brought out Israel from among them, For His mercy *endures* forever;

People:

With a strong hand, and with an outstretched arm, For His mercy *endures* forever;

Leader:

To Him who divided the Red Sea in two, For His mercy *endures* forever;

People:

And made Israel pass through the midst of it, For His mercy *endures* forever;

Leader:

But overthrew Pharaoh and his army in the Red Sea, For His mercy *endures* forever;

People:

To Him who led His people through the wilderness, For His mercy *endures* forever;

Leader:

To Him who struck down great kings, For His mercy *endures* forever;

People:

And slew famous kings, For His mercy *endures* forever —

Leader:

Who rememberd us in our low estate, For His mercy *endures* forever;

People:

And has rescued us from our adveresaries, For His mercy *endures* forever;

Leader:

Who gives food to every creature, For His mercy *endures* forever;

People:

Give thanks to the God of heaven, For His mercy *endures* forever;

"GOING OUT"

Leader:

After Jesus and the disciples concluded their singing of the Hallel Psalms, they "went out."

Now, beloved, go out into the world in peace, knowing that he who has purchased your redemption will present you unto himself in glory at his coming.

The Lord bless you and keep you. The Lord cause his face to shine upon you and be gracious unto you. The Lord turn his face toward you and give you peace, in the name of the Prince of Peace, the Lord Jesus Christ, to whom be glory and praise forever and ever. Amen.

Chapter 9

Passover and Holy Communion

Holy Communion has long been one of the most sacred celebrations in the Christian church. In many churches, it is considered more than a memorial. It is viewed as a sacrament, an outward sign of inward grace or even a visible means of grace. Though it has taken many forms and has been celebrated in various manners, the core of this ceremony is derived from the Passover observance of ancient Israel. At least to some degree, therefore, virtually every Christian congregation or communityalready shares in this rich legacy from biblical and second temple Judaism.

The one ceremony that Jesus instructed his disciples to observe was that of sharing bread and the fruit of the vine in remembrance of his death until his second coming. Indeed, this is the only event in the life of Christ that he requested believers to remember. He did not direct us to remember his birth or his resurrection. He did, however, instruct us to remember his death. Significantly, from the very earliest of church history, Christians have been found faithfully fulfilling our Lord's imperative.

There were two antecedents to the practice of sharing bread and wine that were fulfilled in the homes of the Jewish people even before the time of Jesus. First, there was the Passover celebration wherein the Jews have done precisely as God commanded them by consuming a Passover meal on each anniversary of the first Passover in Egypt wherein they have shared bread and wine. Secondarily, there was the weekly *Shabbat* (Sabbath) meal which also featured the same elements, the bread and the wine, that Jesus employed in instituting communion. While it is clear that Christians, therefore, can remember Christ's death by celebrating communion annually on the day of Passover as Jesus directed, there is no requirement for restricting the celebration to once a year.

NEW COVENANT LITURGY

Following the order which Jesus established on the night of the Last Supper, Paul gave specific instructions to the church: "For I received from the Lord that which I also delivered to you: that the Lord Jesus on the *same* night in which He was betrayed took bread; and when He had given thanks, He broke *it* and said, 'Take, eat; this is My body which is broken for you; do this in remembrance of Me.' In the same manner *He* also *took* the cup after supper, saying, 'This cup is the new covenant in My blood. This do, as often as you drink *it,* in remembrance of Me'" (1 Corinthians 11:23-26).

The immediate antecedent for communion in the earliest church was clearly the Passover *Seder*. The earliest

Christians recognized profound spiritual significance in the death, burial, and resurrection of Jesus around the time of Passover, and they translated that meaning into their ongoing celebration of the biblical festival that was so much a part of their lives and tradition.

The practice of sharing bread and wine in acts of worship was a long-standing tradition among the Hebrew peoples, dating at least to the time of Melchizedek, the priest-king of Salem, who brought forth bread and wine to celebrate Abraham's victory over the marauding pagan kings of Elam, Goyim, Shinar, and Ellasar (Genesis 14:8-20). It continued throughout antiquity, practiced by prophets and kings, by peasants and wise men.

Sharing bread and wine was also manifest in the weekly celebration of *Shabbat* (the Sabbath) in the context of the Jewish home. Just as the annual Passover was primarily a family celebration, so the weekly *Shabbat* was focused in the family. Because the elements of communion were also central to the family *Shabbat* meal that was celebrated in Jewish homes before, during, and after the time of Jesus, communion can be celebrated as a memorial of the rest and peace that are given to believers by the Lord of the Sabbath (Matthew 11:28; 12:8). Indeed, communion can even be celebrated daily by those who desire to do so, and it can also be celebrated in both home or congregation. No clergyperson is required, for it is not necessary to have someone with the authority to "bless" and "consecrate" the bread and the fruit of the vine in order for it to be used for sacred purposes. In reality, every believer is a priest, a part of the priesthood of all believers that functions under the authority of the High Priest, Jesus Christ. Parents, therefore, are free to share communion with their families and friends in the context of their own homes.

Great flexibility is a feature of the Hebraic practice of worship. It is for this reason that various forms may be adopted for celebration of Passover and communion. Both may be combined into one as in the earliest church. What is important is not punctilious, legalistic observance, but remembrance of the pivotal events of biblical history, the Exodus and the death, burial, resurrection, and ascension of Jesus Christ, *Yeshua HaMashiach*.

The following is a liturgy for Holy Communion that incorporates elements of the synagogal liturgy in which Jesus and the apostles participated throughout their lifetimes. It includes the *Shema*, the declaration that Jesus called the first and greatest commandment of the Scriptures. It also incorporates the festival *Amidah*, the full form of which is called "The Prayer" in the synagogue worship experience. It also uses ancient *Berakhah* language patterns for other parts of the ceremony, including the blessings for the bread and the fruit of the vine. This liturgy is filled with Holy Scripture from beginning to end, making it both authoritative and inspirational to the Christian believer.

This ceremony is designed to introduce to liturgical and sacramental congregations the richness of the Hebraic heritage that the church has lost for many centuries. It represents an enrichment of traditional Christian ceremony with language and forms which Jesus and his Jewish family and community employed in their worship of God in home, synagogue, and temple.

This liturgy has been employed in a wide range of Christian communions around the world with outstanding and profoundly meaningful results. Feel free to modify, abbreviate, or expand this outline to contextualize and pesonalize it for your family or community.

Chapter 10

New Covenant Passover

A Liturgy for Holy Communion

PRELUDE

PROCESSIONAL

GREETING:

Leader:
Peace be unto you. The Lord be with you.

People:
And also with you.

CALL TO WORSHIP:

Leader:
Christ our Passover has been sacrificed for us: Christ

has died; Christ is risen; Christ is coming again.

People:

Therefore, let us observe the Festival of Passover.

COLLECT:

Leader:

Almighty God, unto whom all hearts are open, all desires known, and from whom no secrets are hidden, cleanse the thoughts of our hearts by the inspiration of your Holy Spirit, that we may perfectly love you and worthily magnify your holy Name, through Jesus Christ our Lord. Amen.

ACT OF PRAISE: *(Congregation standing)*

(The Act of Praise is modified from the ancient Jewish Amidah *prayer for festivals, a form of which Jesus and the apostles prayed during corporate worship in their synagogues.)*

Leader:

O Lord, open our lips, and our mouths shall declare your praise.

Leader and People:

Blessed are you, O Lord our God and God of our fathers, Abraham, Isaac, and Jacob; the great, mighty and revered God, the Most High God, who bestows loving kindnesses, and is Master of all things; who remembers the pious deeds of the patriarchs, and in love will bring redemption to their children's children for your Name's sake.

Leader:

O King, Helper, Savior, and Shield. Blessed are you, O Lord, the Shield of Abraham.

Leader and People:

You, O Lord, are mighty forever, you revive the dead, you are mighty to save. You sustain the living with loving kindness, revive the dead with great mercy, support the falling, heal the sick, free the bound, and keep your faith to them that sleep in the dust. Who is like unto you, Lord of mighty acts, and who resembles you, O King, who orders death and restores life, and causes salvation to spring forth? Yes, faithful are you to revive the dead. Blessed are you, O Lord, who resurrects the dead.

Leader:

We will sanctify your Name in the world even as they sanctify it in the highest heavens, as it is written by the hand of thy prophet: And they called one unto another and said,

People:

Holy, holy, holy is the Lord of hosts: the whole earth is full of his glory.

Leader:

Those over against them say,

People:

Blessed be the glory of the Lord from his place.

Leader:

And in thy Holy Word it is written, saying,

People:

The Lord shall reign forever; your God, O Zion, unto all generations. Praise ye the Lord.

Leader:

Unto all generations we will declare your greatness, and

to all eternity we will proclaim your holiness. Your praise, O Lord our God, shall not depart from our mouth forever, for you are a great and holy God and King. Blessed are you, O Lord, the holy God.

Leader:

You favor man with knowledge and teach mortals understanding.

People:

You have favored us with a knowledge of your Word and have taught us to perform your will. You have made a distinction, O Lord our God, between holy and profane, between light and darkness, between Israel and the nations, between the Sabbath and the six working days. O our Father, our King, grant that the days which are approaching us may begin for us in peace and that we may be withheld from all sin and cleansed from all iniquity and cleave to the reverence of your name.

Leader and People:

Blessed are you, O Lord our God, who sanctifies Israel and the festive seasons.

Leader:

Accept, O Lord our God, your people Israel and their prayer; restore the service to the inner sanctuary of your house; receive in love and favor both the offerings of Israel and their prayer; and may the worship of your people Israel be ever acceptable unto you.

People:

Our God and God of our fathers! May our remembrance ascend, come, and be accepted before you, with the remembrance of our fathers, of Messiah the Son of David your servant, of Jerusalem your holy city, and of all your people, the house of Israel, bringing deliverance and well-being, grace, loving kindness and mercy, life and peace on this day of the Feast of Unleavened Bread.

Leader and People:

Remember us, O Lord our God, thereon for our well-being; be mindful of us for blessing, and save us unto life: by your promise of salvation and mercy, spare us, and be gracious unto us; have mercy upon us, and save us; for our eyes are bent upon you, because you are a gracious and merciful God and King. Let our eyes behold your return in mercy to Zion. Blessed are you, O Lord, who restores your divine presence unto Zion.

Leader:

We give thanks unto you, for you are the Lord our God and the God of our fathers for ever and ever; you are the Rock of our lives, the Shield of our salvation through every generation.

People:

We will give thanks unto you and declare your praise for our lives which are committed unto your hand, and for our souls which are in your charge, and for your miracles, which are daily with us, and for your wonders and your benefits, which are wrought at all times, evening, morn, and noon. You who are all good, whose mercies fail not, you, merciful God, whose loving kindnesses never cease, we have ever hoped in you.

Leader:

Grant peace, welfare, blessing, grace, loving kindness, and mercy unto us and unto all Israel, your people. Bless us, O our Father, even all of us together, with the light of your countenance; for by the light of your countenance you have given us, O Lord our God, the Word of life, loving kindness and righteousness, blessing, mercy, life, and peace; and may it be good in your sight to bless your people Israel at all times and in every hour with your peace.

Blessed are you, O Lord, who blesses your people Israel with peace.

Leader and People:

O my God! guard my tongue from evil and my lips from speaking guile. Let the words of my mouth and the meditation of my heart be acceptable before you, O Lord, my Rock and my Redeemer. He who makes peace in his high places, may he make peace for us and for all Israel. Amen.

(Songs of praise may also be used to conclude the Act of Praise.)

EXAMINATION:

Leader:

As we prepare to partake of this Feast of the Lord, we are admonished in the Holy Scriptures, "Let a man examine himself, for if we judge ourselves, we should not be judged."

(Silence)

CONFESSION:

Leader:

Most holy and merciful Father, we confess to you and to one another that we have sinned against you by what we have done and by what we have left undone. We have not loved you with our whole heart and mind and strength, and we have not loved our neighbors as ourselves; therefore, we have not had the mind of Christ, and we have grieved you by not using your gifts, by wandering from your ways, and by forgetting your love. Forgive us, we pray you, most merciful Father, as we tarry before you and one another. Renew in us the grace and strength of your Holy Spirit and help us to be perfect in your sight, for the sake of Jesus Christ our Lord and Savior. Amen.

Leader:

My little children, if any man sin, we have an advocate with the Father, Jesus Christ the righteous. Let us, therefore, pray:

Leader and People:

Our Father which art in heaven, hallowed be thy name. Thy kingdom come. Thy will be done in earth as it is in heaven. Give us this day our daily bread, and forgive us our debts as we forgive our debtors. And lead us not into temptation, but deliver us from evil. Amen.

Declaration of Pardon:

Leader:

Blessed are they whose iniquities are forgiven, and whose sins are covered.

Doxology: *(Congregation standing)*

Sermon: *(Appropriate message)*

Affirmation of Faith: *(Congregation standing)*

Leader:

Hear, O Israel, the Lord our God, the Lord is one.

People:

And you shall love the Lord your God with all your heart, and with all your soul, and with all your might. And these words, which I command you this day, shall be upon your heart: and you shall teach them diligently unto your children, and shall talk of them when you sit in your house, and when you walk by the way, and when you lie down, and when you rise up.

Leader and People:

I believe with perfect faith in one God, the Father Almighty, maker of heaven and earth and of all things visible and invisible.

I believe with perfect faith in the Lord Jesus Christ, *Yeshua HaMashiach*, the only begotten Son of God, begotten of his Father before all worlds, God of God, begotten of one substance with the Father; by whom all things were made; who for us men and for our salvation came down from heaven and became incarnate by the Holy Spirit of the virgin Mary and was made man; who was crucified also for us under Pontius Pilate; who suffered and was buried and the third day rose again according to the Scriptures; who ascended into heaven and now sits on the right hand of the Father; and who will come again in power and great glory to judge both the living and the dead in His everlasting kingdom.

I believe with perfect faith in the Holy Spirit, the Lord and giver of life who proceeds from the Father and the Son, who with the Father and the Son together is worshipped and glorified; who spoke by the prophets; and who indwells the hearts of the believers, imparting His gifts and graces.

I believe with perfect faith in the forgiveness of sins, in

the one universal and apostolic congregation of believers, in the resurrection of the body, and in eternal life in the world to come.

HYMN OF WORSHIP: *(An appropriate hymn may be used.)*

OFFERTORY: *(Congregation seated)*

Leader:

Beloved in the Messiah, the Holy Scriptures tell us that after Jesus arose from the dead, he appeared to his disciples and was known to them in the breaking of the bread. Come then to the joyful feast of the Lord. Let us prepare his table with the offerings of our life and labor.

ANTHEM:

(As the offering is received from the congregation, the leaders of the congregation may bring to the the altar the gifts of bread and wine, followed by the offerings that are received from the people.)

OFFERTORY PRAYER:

Leader:

Heavenly Father, receive, we pray you, these offerings of our labor. May *Yeshua*, our great High Priest, be present with us as he was among his disciples, and may we discern his body in the breaking of the bread and his blood in the sharing of the cup. To you be praise and glory with your Son, our Savior, and the Holy Spirit, now and forever. Amen.

DANCE: *(An interpretive dance may be performed.)*

SACRIFICE OF PRAISE AND THANKSGIVING:

Leader:

We are told in the Holy Scriptures that we are built up a spiritual house, a holy priesthood to offer up spiritual sacrifices, acceptable to God by Jesus Christ. Let us, therefore, offer a sacrifice of praise unto God:

Leader:

Our holy Father, almighty and eternal God, we give you thanks always and everywhere, through Jesus Christ your Son our Lord. We bless you for your continual love and care for every creature. We praise you for forming us in your image, and calling us to be your people. Though we rebelled against your love, you did not abandon us in our sin, but sent to us prophets and teachers to lead us into the way of salvation and to teach us to remember your wondrous works through days and feasts of memorial.

Above all, we thank you that in the fullness of time, you gave us the gift of your only begotten Son, who is the way, the truth, and the life. We thank you that He took upon Himself our nature, and by His miraculous birth, His sinless life, His atoning death, and His glorious resurrection, He became our Passover to deliver us from the bondage of sin and death into the hope of everlasting life. We praise you that He now reigns with you in glory and ever lives to intercede for us.

We thank you for the Holy Spirit who leads us into truth, defends us in adversity, and unites us out of every people into one holy and universal church. Therefore, with the whole company of saints here assembled, we worship and glorify you, Eternal God, most holy, and we say with joy and thanksgiving in our hearts:

Leader and People:

Christ our Passover is sacrificed for us. His death we proclaim. His resurrection we declare. His coming we await.

Blessing God for the Bread:

Leader:

Blessed are you, O Lord our God, King of the universe, who brings forth bread from the earth to nourish our bodies, and who brought forth the true bread from heaven to strengthen and establish our souls.

We thank you that in the hour when you had no pleasure in sacrifices and offerings, you did prepared a body of flesh for your only begotten Son and made him a little lower than the angels that he might taste death for all men.

We thank you that he was tempted in all things like as we, yet without sin, that the captain of our salvation was made perfect through suffering, and that he put away sin by the sacrifice of himself.

Now, we remember the New Covenant Passover as we break this bread in which, by the authority of your holy Word, we discern the body of Yeshua the Messiah which was broken for us.

May they who receive this bread be strengthened in their communion with one another and with our Lord Jesus Christ. Amen.

Breaking of the Bread:

Leader:

The bread which we break, is it not the communion of the body of Christ?

People:

Because there is one bread, we who are many are one body in the Messiah, for we all partake of that one spiritual bread.

BLESSING GOD FOR THE CUP:

Leader:

Blessed are you, O Lord our God, King of the universe, who creates the fruit of the vine to confirm and make glad our bodies, and who brought forth the true wine from heaven to indwell our hearts and comfort our spirits.

We thank you that when the blood of bulls and of goats could not make the worshippers perfect, our Savior entered in once into the holy place by his own blood and obtained eternal redemption for us.

Now according to his commandment, we remember the New Covenant Passover as we share this cup in which, by the authority of your holy Word, we discern the blood of Yeshua the Messiah which was shed for the remission of our sins.

May they who receive this cup be strengthened through the fellowship of the Spirit in the union of the body of Christ and the risen Lord. Amen.

RECOGNITION OF THE CUP:

Leader:

The cup which we bless, is it not the communion of the blood of Christ?

People:

The cup which we drink is the New Covenant in the blood of the Messiah.

Prayer for Communicants:

Leader:

Heavenly Father, we pray now that all those who receive of this Passover may be one in communion with the Messiah and one in communion with each other. Grant that they remain faithful in love and hope until that perfect feast with our Lord in the joy of His eternal kingdom. Amen.

Communion:

(The communicants may receive the elements of communion in a variety of ways according to the tradition of the congregation.)

Hymn of Confirmation:

(An appropriate hymn confirming the efficacy of the blood of Christ to atone for sin may be sung.)

Prayer of Thanksgiving: *(Congregation standing)*

Leader and People:

Almighty and everlasting God, we give you thanks for receiving our sacrifice of praise and thanksgiving, and for feeding us with the spiritual food of the body and blood of our Savior Jesus Christ. Strengthen us ever with your Holy Spirit that we may serve you in faith and love, by word and deed, until we come to the joy of your eternal kingdom; through Yeshua HaMashiach, our Lord, who lives and reigns with you and the same Holy Spirit, now and forever. Amen.

HYMNS OF FELLOWSHIP:

(Songs stressing the unity of the body of Christ may be sung, and appropriate gestures of fellowship may be exchanged among the communicants.)

HYMN OF EXPECTATION:

(A hymn emphasizing the coming of the Messiah may be sung.)

BENEDICTION:

Leader:

Now the God of peace, that brought again from the dead our Lord Jesus, that great shepherd of the sheep, through the blood of the everlasting covenant, make you perfect in every good work to do His will, working in you that which is well pleasing in His sight. The Lord bless you and keep you. The Lord make his face to shine upon you and be gracious unto you. The Lord lift up his countenance upon you and give you peace, through *Yeshua HaMashiach*, our Lord; to whom be glory for ever and ever, world without end. Amen.

The Dismissal:

Leader:

Go out into the world in peace. Be strong and of good courage. Hold fast what is good. Love and serve the Lord, rejoicing in the power of the Holy Spirit.

Recessional

Postlude

Chapter 11

Shall We Now Observe the Festival?

Both in history and in the present time, many Jewish and Christian leaders offer considerable objection to Christian observance of the Passover. It seems that neither official Judaism nor official Christianity is very undertanding of Christians who seem to confuse and confound the clear distinctions between these two faiths by attempting to observe the traditional Passover, with or without including the Calvary experience.

Christian Concerns

Most Christian objection to Passover observance is based on ecclesiastical anti-Judaism that developed after the church's first century. Before the church fully opened the door to the Gentiles at the Jerusalem Council, the vast majority of its communicants were Jews; therefore, there was no question as to whether or not followers of Christ should observe Passover. Its celebration was a significant part of the Jewish heritage upon which the early Jewish leaders of the church had founded a faith and polity that recognized Jesus as the fulfillment of the messianic expectation of his people and as the Savior of the world.

As Gentiles came to prominence in the church, however, they were influenced by traditions which they had brought with them and by pressures from the political powers of the day to disassociate themselves from the Jews and things Jewish. At the same time a controversy raged in the church over whether or not in addition to faith in Jesus complete obedience to the law of Moses was essential to salvation. Of particular concern was the practice of circumcision, whether it should be physically enforced on new converts to this Judeo-Christianity or whether the circumcision of the heart that God had described to Moses, Jeremiah, and Paul was sufficient without the physical procedure.

In some of Paul's writings, he openly attacked those in the Jewish community (both in traditional Judaism and in the church) who believed that salvation resulted from submission to and ritual observance of God's law. This social criticism was initially an intramural argument among fellow Jews; however, it was widely misunderstood and generalized by later Gentile church leaders.

Rather than maintaining Paul's balanced position on the interrelationship of Christian faith and the law, subsequent church leaders adopted an increasingly antinomian posture, ultimately insisting that Christians have nothing in common with Jews and Judaism. This was particularly true in relationship to ecclesiastical holy days which had been changed from their original first-century construct to accommodate the various societies into which the Christian faith had expanded. Passages such as Colossians 2:16-17 were enlisted to assure Christians that all "Jewish" holy days and sabbaths had been abandoned by the church.

Additionally, virtually all of the Christian church, including the reform movements that began in the sixteenth century and afterward, maintained a supersessionist view toward Jews and Judaism in which they asserted that Christianity had forever replaced Judaism in God's economy of salvation and that Christians had forever replaced the Jewish people who had been cut off from salvation and cursed because of their rejection of Jesus.

Having been ripped from its moorings, Christianity drifted on the tide of human tradition, often swirling in the maelstrom of a pagan-based worldview that allowed such violent conduct toward the Jewish people. In this kind of environment, it was unthinkable that a Christian would celebrate a "Jewish" festival, including the Passover. Even today, in an age of enlightenment, much of the church remains wary of any involvement in "Jewish" practices.

Growing numbers of Christians, however, are rejecting these historical arguments and are rediscovering Christianity's Jewish connection. They are saying to themselves, "If it was right for Jesus and the apostles, it must be right for me." They are embracing teachings and practices that were clearly a part of the first century church's system of praise, worship, and service. And, they are discovering rewarding and fulfilling experiences as they immerse themselves in this thoroughly biblical and "New Testament" heritage.

CHRISTIAN PASSOVER–A JEWISH INTERPRETATION

Both Jews and Christians need to recognize the fact that Christian understanding of prophecies and practices in the Hebrew Scriptures rests on interpretations of those

Scriptures by Jews of the first century who came to see in Jesus of Nazareth the Messiah of Israel. Jesus himself was a Torah-observant Jew. All of the apostles on whom the church was built were Torah-observant Jews. Virtually the entire constituency of the church's first decade was made up of Jewish believers who were faithful to the law. Indeed, many of their number were and continued to be Pharisees (Acts 15:5) and temple priests (Acts 6:7). As Jews, they had a clear and distinct right to interpret their Scriptures apart from any overarching dogma or systematic theology imposed upon them by another part of the traditional Jewish community, for no one branch of Judaism was dominant at that time.

Christian interpretations of the Passover and its manifestation in the death and resurrection of Jesus are established on the solid rock of *Jewish* interpretation. These Jewish followers of Jesus celebrated the Passover *Seder* traditions of their day, imbuing each part with additional meaning from the life, death, resurrection, and ascension of Jesus. When the early Jewish leaders of the Christian church interpreted the Passover events allegorically as pointing to Jesus, they did so on the basis of the hermeneutics of Jewish sages and rabbis. Later Gentile Christian allegorical interpretations of the Exodus Passover events merely expanded upon the foundation that their Jewish predecessors had laid. These ideas, then, were birthed in the fertile hearts of observant Jews: Jesus and his apostles. They are, therefore, Jewish interpretations, not Gentile interpolations that can be casually dismissed as lacking authenticity.

NATURALIZED CITIZENS

One of the key concepts that was advanced when the Jewish founders of the Christian church purposed to open the door of faith to the Gentiles was that this action was also a fulfillment of the Hebrew Scriptures, which had predicted that Israel's light would be carried to the nations of the world (Isaiah 42:6; 49:6; cf. Luke 2:32; Acts 13:47). It was also a cardinal principle that all those Gentiles who were added to the church were, in effect, added to the commonwealth of Israel (Ephesians 2:12-16) or the tabernacle of David (Acts 15:15-18), albeit on the basis of less restrictive initiation requirements.

The bottom line is that all the Gentiles who came to faith in Jesus were considered by their Jewish brethren to have been grafted into God's family tree of salvation and covenant relationship (the theme of Romans 11). They were also considered to have become naturalized citizens in the commonwealth or nation of Israel, a teaching clearly set forth in Ephesians 2. They were "no more strangers and foreigners" but "fellow citizens with the saints and of the same body." Even in ancient Israel, a proselyte was to be considered as though he had been born to Jewish parents. Gentiles who had become disciples of Rabbi Jesus were recognized as a part of the "Israel of God."

Paul made this clear in 1 Corinthians 10:1 when, writing specifically to Gentile Christians, he declared: "For I do not want you to be ignorant of the fact, brothers, that *our* forefathers were all under the cloud and that they all passed through the sea" (emphasis added). Coupled with his declaration to Gentile believers in Romans 4:12, 16 that Abraham is "the father of us all [Jew and Gentile]," it is clear that the apostle considered the Gentiles who had come to faith in the Messiah to be children of the patriarch, Abraham.

With this in mind, it is only natural that there is a longing in the heart of Christians to rediscover the roots of their faith, to find their way back home. Clearly Gentiles by birth, they have been added to the nation of Israel by faith in Jesus. As fellow citizens with the saints of Israel, they are no more "Gentiles in the flesh" (Ephesians 2:11). They are, therefore, entitled to the entire heritage of God's chosen people. If one immigrates into a nation of the modern world, he can either remain a foreigner or he can go through the process of naturalization. In the United States when one takes the oath of allegiance, he is as much a citizen as the person whose ancestors signed the Declaration of Independence, and he has essentially the same rights. Virtually every other nation has a memorial day to celebrate its statehood, and naturalized citizens share equally with the native born in that celebration.

Passover is the yearly memorial of the liberation of Israel, the event that set them on the path toward Sinai and their incorporation as God's chosen nation of priests. Passover, then, is foundational to Judaism, but it is also foundational to Christianity, for if there had been no Passover, there would have been no Israel to have produced Jesus, nor would there have been a nation of Israel into whom Gentile believers could be added as naturalized citizens.

It is only natural, therefore, that every Christian should have a deep-seated sense of connection with the profoundly theological, yet solidly historical events of salvation history. All salvation history, including that detailed in the Hebrew Scriptures, is relative to all Christians. It is a central part of the Hebraic heritage of the Christian faith that has been obscured by centuries of Hellenization and Latinization of the teachings of Jesus and the apostles.

THE INEVITABILITY OF RESTORATION

The good news is that God has designed a reformation of restoration for the Christian church that is utterly inevitable because it is supported by the infallible prophetic Word of God. Peter made it very clear that the time of the coming of the Messiah will be a time of restoration: "And he shall send Jesus Christ, who before was preached unto you: whom heaven must receive until the period of restoration of all things about which God spoke by the mouth of his holy prophets from ancient time" (Acts 3:20-21, KVJ, NASB). This prophetic pronouncement speaks of the yet future event when the Messiah himself will return to restore all things that the prophets have predicted; however, it also speaks of what will essentially be a day of preparation for the Sabbatical Millennium, a time when human beings will join in concert with God to effect the restoration of his divine purposes for his people.

This will be a further unfolding of the Jewish concept of *tikkun olam*, the "restoration of the earth," wherein God partners with his children to restore what has been polluted or destroyed by the power of sin and rebellion against the Almighty. This restoration will take place first in a spiritual dimension in which everything that the prophets and apostles set forth that has subsequently been overwhelmed by human tradition will once again emerge to be embraced and practiced by Christians everywhere. Then, the restoration will take on physical and universal dimensions when the Messiah, Jesus, returns to restore and renew all things and establish the universal dominion of God over all the earth.

Nothing can prevent the unfolding of these profound

prophetic events as the timetable that God has established for their fulfillment signals their arrival on the human scene. Everything that has been lost by erosion or by the accretions and encroachments of human aberrations will be fully restored to its former pristine glory. The gold of God's truth will be recovered from the dust and grime of human traditions. The treasures of Holy Scripture will be rediscovered and restored to their first glory, and the people of God will be enriched by the renewed connection with the faith of the Hebrew prophets, sages, and apostles.

Further good news is that this amazing prophetic work of restoration and renewal is already happening. As a matter of fact, in a measure it has been under way since the turn of the sixteenth century when a movement of "Christain Hebraists" was inspired to return to the Hebrew Sciptures, to the Hebrew language, and to the history and culture of the Jewish people in order to understand and practice their faith as God had intended it in the beginning.

The work of restoration only grows stronger every day. What began with a handful of people now encompasses millions around the world. The inevitability of restoration throughout the Christian church is as certain as the rise of dough when the leavening agent is present in bread. The restoration truth that God has released into the church and the world will continue to advance until the whole of the church, Israel, and the world is impacted by the divine word and work of reformation and renewal.

This is a distinctive work of the Holy Spirit, the one who permeates the entire Christian church by indwelling the hearts of believers everywhere. It is a sovereign work of divine purpose that has no single identifiable earthly source and is not being orchestrated by any single earthly individual or organization. It is a work of God, an unfolding of divine purpose. It is a work in which the Father seeks those who will worship him in spiritual truth (John 4:23). And what the Father seeks, he will find! As Henry Wadsworth Longfellow lyrically said, "The wrong will fail, the right prevail, with peace on earth, good will to men." All that Satan has polluted will be cleaned up; everything that he has destroyed will be restored. God will have things as he intended in the beginning. Truth will stand when the worlds are on fire. In the face of such inevitability, why would anyone not want to search out the original paths, find the good way, and walk therein (Jeremiah 6:16)? The pure in heart will see God and walk in his ways.

To Celebrate or Not to Celebrate

Should Christians celebrate Passover? This is a legitimate question to which much of the church and most of Judaism have said no. But, the answer for believers must be what is given in Holy Scripture, not in human traditions.

Why should Christians celebrate Passover? When we remain faithful to the Bible, the answer is clear and unequivocal: "Because Christ our Passover has been sacrificed for us; therefore, let us observe the festival [Passover and Unleavened Bread] . . . with the unleavened bread of sincerity and truth." This directive is from a Christian apostle who even then was still a Jewish rabbi, and he gave it to Gentiles. What could possibly be more apparent?

The next question is, How should Christians observe the Passover? Again, the Bible gives a clear answer. What better example could we have than that of our Lord Jesus himself? According to the Gospels, he celebrated the Passover with his disciples in the traditional *Seder* that the sages had prescribed for his time. The core of the modern *seder* predates the time of Christ and was the order which Jesus employed in the Last Supper. Christians are free to imitate Jesus' way of life at any time; however, they are bound to no specific ritual for their salvation. Freedom in the Messiah permits great flexibility of practice.

Should any remain confused, Paul gives the liturgical order for recognizing Calvary in the Passover celebration: "For I received from the Lord that which I also delivered to you: that the Lord Jesus on the same night in which he was betrayed took bread; and when he had given thanks, he broke *it* and said, 'Take, eat; this is my body which is broken for you; do this in remembrance of me.' In the same manner he also took the cup after supper, saying, 'This cup is the new covenant in my blood. This do, as often as you drink it, in remembrance of me.' For as often as you eat this bread and drink this cup, you proclaim the Lord's death till he comes" (1 Corinthians 11:23-26).

Passover? Celebrate!

Featuring Informative, Challenging Books by
Dr. John D. Garr

Our Lost Legacy is a provocative, inspiring primer on the Jewish roots of the Christian faith. This volume presents selected essays in which Dr. Garr urges the church to recover its Hebrew heritage. These pages call Christians back to the Bible, to the roots of faith and a more comprehensive understanding of their Hebrew Lord.
240 pages, ISBN 0-96782797-2-2.

God and Women: Woman in God's Image and Likeness is a comprehensive, scholarly examination of the way in which God created women. These pages will take you back to the beginning when God created male and female coequal and consubstantial, designed to display the image of God to all of creation.
320 pages, ISBN 978-0-9794514-4-7.

Blessings for Family and Friends provides you with solid information about God's blessing system and with demonstrations and examples of blessings that you can pronounce over your family and friends for all occasions. This is a spectacular gift book that you will want to keep for yourself. Amazing blessings await you in this book.
160 pages, ISBN 978-0-9794514-3-0.

The Hem of His Garment discusses the context of the woman who was healed when she touched the hem of Jesus' garment. You will simply be amazed at the great impact that the ancient Jewish tradition of attaching fringes to the four corners of their mantles had upon the lives of biblical people, including this woman.
160 pages, ISBN 0-96782797-0-6.

Living Emblems will help you understand the biblical symbols that were designed by God and by his people Israel. Each emblem is full of rich insight that points to the person and work of the Messiah, Jesus. Recognizing these spiritual truths is a profound means of underscoring the truth of Christianity's Jewish connection.
160 pages, ISBN 096782797-1-4.

God's Lamp, Man's Light is a masterful analysis of the menorah, the only biblical symbol that has the distinction of being designed by God himself. As you read this book, you will be amazed at the wealth of insight that has been hidden from the historical church because of its separation from Judaism and things Jewish.
160 pages, ISBN 0-9678279-4-9.

Family Sanctuary is a provocative look at the modern home that offers clear answers for families in crisis and for those who want to restore their families to biblical foundations. Reading this book will be a life-changing experience for you and for your family as you learn to walk in the blessings of biblical family life.
160 pages, ISBN 096782748-1.

Bless You! is a systematic, comprehensive study of the biblically Hebraic concept of blessing and its impact in the lives of believers from ancient times until today. This powerful dynamic can now be experienced in every Christian home. You can restore this vital part from the Hebraic faith of Jesus and the apostles.
160 pages, ISBN 096782797-7-3.

Order From
HEBRAIC CHRISTIAN GLOBAL COMMUNITY
P.O. Box 421218
Atlanta, Georgia 30342, U.S.A.
www.HebraicCommunity.org

Hebraic Heritage Christian Center is an institution of higher education that is dedicated to the vision of restoring a Hebraic model for Christian education. A consortium of scholars, spiritual leaders, and business persons, the Center features a continually developing curriculum in which each course of study is firmly anchored in the Hebrew foundations of the Christian faith.

The Hebraic Heritage Christian Center vision combines both the ancient and the most modern in an educational program that conveys knowledge, understanding, and wisdom to a world-wide student population. The Center seeks to restore the foundations of original Christianity in order to equip its students with historically accurate, theologically sound understanding of the biblical faith that Jesus and the apostles instituted and practiced. At the same time the Center endeavors to implement the finest in innovative, cutting-edge technology in a distance-learning program that delivers its user-friendly courses by the Internet.

Among the wide range of services and products that Hebraic Heritage Christian Center offers are the publications of Hebraic Heritage Press. These are delivered both in traditional print media as well as in electronic media to serve both the Center's student population and the general public with inspiring and challenging materials that have been developed by the Center's team of scholars.

Those who are interested in sharing in the development of Hebraic Heritage Christian Center and its commitment to restoring the Jewish roots of the Christian faith are invited to join the Founders' Club, people who support this team of scholars and leaders by becoming co-founders of this institution. Many opportunities for endowments are also available to those who wish to create a lasting memorial to the cause of Christian renewal and Christian-Jewish rapprochement.